SKIP MARTIN

Twelve Plays for Christmas

... but not a Partridge in a Pear Tree

Dramas About the Gift of Christmas

WestBow Press books may be ordered through booksellers or by contacting:

WestBow Press
A Division of Thomas Nelson & Zondervan
1663 Liberty Drive
Bloomington, IN 47403
www.westbowpress.com
1 (866) 928-1240

ISBN: 978-1-4908-7918-5 (sc)
ISBN: 978-1-4908-7917-8 (e)

Library of Congress Control Number: 2015907098

Print information available on the last page.

WestBow Press rev. date: 06/18/2015

To my wife
BETH MARTIN
without whom none of the dramas
in this book would ever have been written

Contents

Foreword

By the Rev. Dan Cracchiola
Grace Church, Sarasota, Florida

Galatians 6:14
"May I never boast except in the cross of our Lord Jesus Christ"

Twenty two years ago I had the honor of taking over the leadership of the Singing Christmas Tree for the First Baptist Church of Sarasota, Florida. At that time the Tree had already been a Sarasota tradition for nineteen years, but I had a desire to change the face of the program and make it have even more of an impact on the Sarasota community. One of the ways I felt we could do that was adding drama to our program. God responded by blessing First Baptist Church with a group of talented people who helped turn the Singing Christmas Tree into a vehicle to reach the people in our community for Christ.

Skip Martin was one of those people. For more than twenty years Skip wrote and developed scripts which would help lead people to Jesus, by combining the right mix of seriousness and humor to deliver a powerful message. For twenty years Skip was right on target. The scripts in this book are some of the best Christian scripts I have ever read. You would do well to consider any of the scripts in this book for your Christmas program, Singing Christmas Tree or other church event.

Dan Cracchiola

Acknowledgments

I wish to express my thanks and gratitude to the following people for their help with this publication and each of the dramas it contains.

To Dan Cracchiola for your great patience and for your faith that somehow every year the script would finally get done just in the nick of time. Your leadership and the evidence of your faith has been a real inspiration to me. You have been a real blessing to me over the years.

To Mark Woodland who helped me, literally, write some of the scenes, and who rewrote them on stage nightly during performances. You have been a marvelous fountain of ideas and I truly have been blessed to have worked with such a gifted actor for so many years.

To Sherry Erb for your wonderful creativity and thoughts. As you know, some of your ideas were the source of some of these scripts. You energized me when I needed it.

To Maxine Strock for the tremendous job you did of copyediting this book. Your assistance was invaluable. You provided me with a great peace of mind.

To all of the choir members of the Singing Christmas Tree who gave me their ideas, feedback, and encouragement through the years. You helped me immeasurably.

To my parents, Benjamin G. Martin and Mariel Oliver, for your encouragement of me as a young teen by taking me to the theater and for supporting my budding interest in drama. You prepared me for writing these dramas.

To my daughters, Allison Martin and Ashleigh Martin, who were always my first critics. You patiently endured when bits and pieces of your personalties were written into dramas which were performed in front of thousands of people. You have enriched me throughout your lives.

To my wife, Beth Martin, who was a constant source of inspiration for the more than twenty years during which I wrote these and other dramas. You reviewed, you critiqued, you suggested, and you encouraged. Perhaps most important, you patiently endured while I took a two year hiatus from practicing law in order to attend film school. You have sustained me for twenty seven years.

Preface

When I obtained a Masters in Fine Arts from the Florida State University School of Motion Picture, Television and Recording Arts in 1991, I never imagined the pathway which would lead to the publication of this book. I was very fortunate to learn a little about script writing at FSU from talented writers such as Stuart Kaminsky, the well known writer and screenwriter, who lived in Sarasota, Florida at that time. Already a practicing attorney when I started film school, I had hopes of writing and developing scripts for narrative films which could be produced by filmmakers in the then struggling Christian film industry. Unfortunately, the advent of the DVD made the production of narrative Christian films economically unfeasible during the 90's. But as I discovered, when one door is closed, another door is opened.

It was during a casual conversation between Dan Cracchiola and my wife, that Dan became aware that I had some training in script writing. The rest is history. I began writing scripts to be used by First Baptist Church of Sarasota in its annual production of The Singing Christmas Tree. I was privileged to have this opportunity for more than twenty years, and what an incredible twenty years it was. Dan shared my belief that Christian drama could be one of the most effective ways of sharing the message of Christ with others. We believed that the combination of a well written story with interesting characters and talented actors, with beautiful and inspiring music, would lead to a synergy which would have a powerful impact on audiences.

The twelve scripts in this publication have each been successfully performed multiple times before a total audience of more than 10,000 people as part of the annual Singing Christmas Tree production of First Baptist Church of Sarasota. They have been tried and tested. Two of these dramas have been performed at other churches in or near our area: Faith Baptist Church in Sarasota, and First Baptist Church of Brandon, Florida. One of those churches presented the drama as part of a Singing Christmas Tree program; the other did not. Additionally, another two of these dramas were performed in Manchester, England and Wiesbaden, Germany by First Baptist Church members. The basic format used in all of these performances was for the various acts of the drama to be performed with one, two, or sometimes three songs performed between each act. Sometimes the music performed would have a strong connection to the scene it preceded or followed, sometimes it did not. Toward the end of each performance, before the last song, our pastor would enter the stage and give a short five minute message.

Either way, the combination of drama and music and short message seemed to always have a beneficial impact.

These dramas are not just cute stories with a general Christmas theme. Rather, each of these dramas was written with the express intention of presenting the good news about the Gift of Christmas in a unique way. Humor, I believe, is one of the most effective ways to engage and relax an audience. So humor was liberally incorporated in these dramas whenever possible. But ultimately each drama was always written with the goal of leading the unsuspecting audience member at least part of the way down the pathway toward accepting and knowing Christ. As Christians we are all called to be witnesses, and with these dramas, I have attempted, with God's grace, to answer that call.

The question of whether to require royalties for production of these dramas was a delicate problem for me. Ultimately, my hope is to have these dramas, and the message they portray, performed for as many people as possible. This means some marketing and promotion will be required. Yet, the successful publication, marketing and promotion of these plays has a monetary cost. Accordingly, I have chosen to request a small royalty in conjunction with the performance of any of these dramas in order to help defray that cost. Royalty information and an application form can be found near the end of this book. I hope that you will understand this choice and will join me in this endeavor to present to the lost, the glorious message of our Lord and Savior Jesus Christ.

Humbly,
Skip Martin

Holiday at the Inn

By Skip Martin

<u>OVERTURE</u>: Music only

Scene 1

LIGHTS COME UP to reveal the open lobby of a small New England inn. It is a very simple room with primary features consisting of the front desk and a large bear skin rug in the center of the room.

PAUL enters with his arms full of firewood.

PAUL

Marie...Marie. Better hurry, the storm's gonna be here soon. *(After a considerable pause, there is no answer)* How d'ya like that. If this were her calling, and I didn't answer, how long do you think it would be before I would hear the end of it? (*Shouts musically*) MAR-I-E!

MARIE enters from behind PAUL.

MARIE

(Yelling back from behind Paul)

I can hear you.

PAUL

(Drops the logs)

What the...?

MARIE

Oh...Paul. I spent at least a half an hour washing that floor this morning. Can you please clean that up. What if some guests walked in?

PAUL

Guests? What guests? This place is as empty as a Bill Clinton promise.[1]

MARIE

Paul, where's your faith? Remember, "Faith is being sure of what we hope for and..."

PAUL

"...certain of what we do not see." All right, all right, I'll clean it up. I've just about finished with this firewood here.

MARIE

Now, what is this nonsense about a storm? I was just outside. Looked perfectly fine to me.

PAUL

Well, there's a storm coming. I can feel it in my bones. Mark my words.

MARIE

You always say that you can feel some...weather or another in your bones.

PAUL

Yes, and I'm always right too.

MARIE

Well, for once, I hope you are right. I don't think we've ever had a Christmas Eve without having had at least one good snow.

PAUL

No. And no snow, no guests...

---

1 This drama was originally written in the 90's when William J. Clinton was president. Feel free to use the name of your favorite politician of either political party here.

TROOPER TOM enters.

TROOPER TOM

...and no one stuck in their cars.

MARIE

Hello, Tom. Can I get you a cup of coffee?

TROOPER TOM

Thanks, but no thanks. I just got a weather bulletin. Looks like you're gonna get your snow.

PAUL smiles smugly and looks at MARIE.

MARIE

Yes, we know. We got the news from Paul's bones.

TROOPER TOM

Huh?

MARIE

Just an inside joke.

TROOPER TOM

Ah. Well..uh...I'm on my way to put barricades up on the pass. If you get anyone passing by, can you tell them that the Highway Patrol recommends that they stay off the roads until this thing blows over?

PAUL

Righto.

TROOPER TOM exits.

PAUL

Well, one more load and that oughta do it.

MARIE

Looks wonderful Paul. You sure do know how to make a warm fire.

PAUL

With someone like you to light it dear, it's the easiest thing in the world.

PAUL and MARIE laugh and give each other a warm hug.

MARIE

I do hope we get some guests soon. It just wouldn't seem like Christmas without telling the wonderful story of the Christ child. I pray that this year we'll have someone who has never heard the real Christmas story before.

PAUL

Better pray really hard.

MARIE

Oh, you of little faith. I'm going to check the mail.

PAUL

Okay.

MARIE EXITS.

PAUL

(Looking both ways)

C'mon Bear. Let's go for a walk.

PAUL picks up a leash which is attached to the bear skin rug, which is actually a costume with an actor inside of it. He tugs on the leash and the bear raises up on four legs and follows PAUL offstage.

PAUL and BEAR EXIT.

LIGHTS FADE OUT.

<u>SONG</u>

<u>SONG</u>

Scene 2

LIGHTS COME UP.

BOB and DENISE enter along with their ten year old daughter ALICE.

BOB

Hello? Hello?

PAUL

Can I help you?

DENISE

We're lost.

BOB

No. We are not lost. I'm just not used to going this way.

DENISE

We're lost.

PAUL

Where are you headed?

ALICE

We're going to Grandma's house.

DENISE

That's in Handale.

PAUL

Well you can get there by taking State Road here right up through the pass.

BOB

This is State Road? I thought this was the highway bypass.

PAUL

The bypass? Goodness no. That's forty miles back down the road. You must have taken a wrong turn back in Greenburg.

DENISE

I am not going to say I told you so.

BOB

(To Paul) Right...twenty years from now she'll still be telling me about it. *(To Denise)* Tell you what. Why don't you drive? You've had plenty of practice driving from the back seat.

ALICE

They were fighting like this the whole way.

DENISE

We were not fighting. We were just having a little discussion.

PAUL

Well, if you folks don't mind a little advice....the Highway Patrol was just here. They're recommending that everyone stay off the roads on account of the storm.

BOB

You call this a storm? Nothing but a few snowflakes.

DENISE

I don't know Bob. Maybe we should?

PAUL

You're welcome to stay here. Our best room is available and tomorrow morning we're having a great Christmas spread.

BOB

Well thank you, but we're already behind schedule. Besides we're not that big on Christmas.

PAUL

Well, even if you're not big on Christmas, you really should reconsider...

BOB

(Taking Alice's hand)

Thanks, 'preciate it. But we really need to get going.

Just three more hours and we'll be there.

DENISE

(Shrugs)

Looks like we're going. Hope you have a happy Christmas.

PAUL and MARIE walk them to the door.

PAUL and MARIE

Bye. Drive carefully.

LIGHTS FADE OUT.

<u>SONG</u>

Scene 3

LIGHTS COME UP.

TROOPER TOM enters and strides over to the desk and rings the bell. PAUL enters.

TROOPER TOM

Looks like I've got some customers for you. Tried to get past the barricades and I had to pull them out of a drift.

PAUL, DENISE, and ALICE enter with their arms full of suitcases. They are tired, heavily bundled, and covered with snow.

DENISE

Bob...

BOB

Don't say it...don't say it.

PAUL

Let me help you with those.

MARIE

Paul will take you to your room. But as soon as you get freshened up you'll want to hurry back down. We've got a special house coffee, hot chocolate, and the warmest fire on this side of the mountains.

LIGHTS FADE OUT.

<u>SONG</u>

Scene 4

LIGHTS COME UP.

ALL are seated in the parlor. MARIE is serving coffee and hot chocolate.

ALICE

Mmmmmm. This is the best.

DENISE

Coffee's...quite good.

BOB

Not bad.

PAUL

Marie has a special recipe. Passed down for generations.

MARIE

It's one of our Christmas traditions.

ALICE

I like Christmas! But we don't really believe in it. My Dad says it's like the Tooth Fairy.

BOB

Well it's all commercialized now. Nothing but shopping and a way of getting further into debt.

MARIE

Yes. We seem to have forgotten what Christmas is really all about.

DENISE

When I was a little girl, I remember that my father would go out into the woods and cut down a nice big evergreen. Now that's a real Christmas. It was a really nice tradition.

MARIE

Like singing Christmas carols.

DENISE

That too. That's one of my favorite memories.

PAUL

We have a tradition here at the lodge that we would like to share with you. Every year we gather all the lodge guests around the fireplace and tell a wonderful story. Alice, have you ever heard the story of Christmas?

ALICE

You mean like Rudolph the Red-Nosed Reindeer?

PAUL

(Chuckles)

We'll not exactly. It's a story about a Christmas baby.

ALICE

I like stories.

PAUL

Folks, what'd'ya say?

BOB

I don't know, its getting late.

DENISE

Oh why not, Bob? Relax. We're here now so we might as well enjoy our stay.

BOB

All right.

PAUL

Good. Now, Alice, the story of Christmas begins a very long, long time ago in a tiny land called Israel. The people there were like people all around the world today. They were stubborn; they were proud; and they were quite sinful. You see, God had given them some commandments, telling them to love Him and to love one another. But they just couldn't seem to obey Him. I guess He seemed too far away, and they just didn't understand what He was like.

ALICE

I don't understand what God is like either. Sometimes I think he's kinda mean.

PAUL

Well I guess maybe the people of Israel, the Jews, felt just like you. So God, in heaven, had a plan. He decided to send as much of Himself as He could to our world and to become a man. And as a man, He could show us and teach us what He was really like.

ALICE

How could God be two places at once?

PAUL

(Chuckles)

You and I certainly couldn't do that; but remember this is God, and with God everything is possible. Well, where was I? Ah, yes. When the right time came,

God and man became one in the form of Jesus. And He was born as a little baby, just like you and I, in a town called Bethlehem.

ALICE

Were there lots of people there waiting for Him?

PAUL

Only a few. You see, out in the fields near Bethlehem, there were some shepherds, who were watching over their sheep. It was a quiet night, just like any other, when suddenly an angel appeared before them, and then a whole host of angels. And then the angels began singing a song.

LIGHTS FADE OUT.

<u>SONG</u>

Scene 5

LIGHTS COME UP.

ALICE

Wow. What did they do when they saw all those angels?

BOB

There is no such thing as angels, honey.

DENISE

How do you know? Just because you've never seen one doesn't mean they don't exist.

BOB

I'd have to see one before I'd believe it.

PAUL

Well Alice, the shepherds did what I think anybody would do. They went to find this baby. They ran through the streets of Bethlehem, telling anyone they passed about what they had seen. And they found this baby, about whom the angels sang, in the humblest of surroundings. There with Him in a stable were His mother, Mary, and father, Joseph.

LIGHTS FADE OUT.

<u>SONG</u>

<u>SONG</u>

<u>SONG</u>

Scene 7

LIGHTS COME UP.

ALICE

Can we sing some Christmas songs?

MARIE

That's a wonderful idea.

DENISE

Come on, Bob. You have a great voice.

BOB

(Reluctantly)

Ah, I was just getting settled in...

ALICE

Please, please, daddy?

PAUL

You don't have to know the words; we have some song sheets.

BOB

All right.

PAUL

That's the spirit.

MARIE

This is going to be fun!

PAUL then turns to the audience and invites them to join the carol sing.

PAUL

(Hands out handouts)

(To Cast and audience) Ok everybody, the words are in these handouts that we're handing out, so everybody join together and sing with us, nice and loud.

LIGHTS FADE OUT.

<u>SONG</u> *(A carol medley)*

Scene 8

LIGHTS COME UP.

PAUL

More coffee anyone?

BOB

No. Thank you.

DENISE

Just a little.

MARIE

(To Paul)

I'll get it.

ALICE

That was fun!

DENISE

Reminds me of when I was a little girl.

ALICE

Did baby Jesus get any birthday presents?

PAUL

As a matter of fact He did. After Jesus was born, wise men, called Magi, came from a land to the east. They followed a star, which appeared before them and led them to Bethlehem and to the house where this child, the Christ was. The Magi were overjoyed, and they bowed down and worshiped Him. Then they gave Him treasures and presented Him with gifts of gold, and incense, and myrrh.

LIGHTS FADE OUT.

<u>SONG</u>

Scene 9

LIGHTS COME UP.

DENISE

That must be how Christmas giving started.

PAUL

In part yes, but part of our Christmas giving came from the pagan holidays.

BOB

That I believe.

PAUL

It's true that Christmas has become commercialized Bob. But giving is an important part of Christmas. You see with the birth of Jesus, God gave us the ultimate gift. The gift of a Savior who came into this world, and through a life of truth and grace, showed us what God is really like.

BOB

Jesus may have been a great teacher, but did it do any good? I mean look around you in this world. Besides if He was God's son, why did God let Him die such a miserable death?

PAUL

That's the part that makes Christmas so wonderful. You see a person who has sin, cannot live in the presence of God because God is so Holy. Can you think of anyone who has lived a perfect life, without sin?

BOB

Well...how 'bout...maybe...no.

PAUL

Ah, that was God's problem. No one could live in His presence, because no one is without sin. If He could only take away people's sin. The solution, you see, was Jesus. this little baby in Bethlehem, whom we call God's Son. When Jesus grew up, He had a ministry of teaching and healing for three years. Then when the time came, He gave up his life, voluntarily, dying a horrible death on a cross, in order to take onto Himself all of mankind's sin. The Bible tells us that if we accept the gift of Jesus' life, and place our faith in Him, believing that He is the One whom God has sent for our salvation, that we will be able to have eternal life in God's presence.

BOB

I don't think I've ever heard it explained this way before.

ALICE

Can I accept Jesus gift?

DENISE

Yes, you can honey. You know, a long time ago I was confirmed, but I really didn't understand it like I do now.

PAUL

It's really quite simple, all you have to do to accept the gift of Jesus, is to believe in Him by faith, and then let Him take over your life.

BOB

Do you mean that I can just decide for God to take over my life, and can tell Him so, as matter-of-factly as that, and have it work?

PAUL

That's right. Do it as matter-of-factly as you please. You don't have to have all of your theological beliefs sorted out. Nor do you have to understand everything. You just come to Christ as you are. Questions, contradictions, doubts, everything. You make a definite decision of the will toward Him. After that the next move is up to Him. The feelings, the proof that He has heard, even the understanding will come later.

DENISE

I'd like to do that. Is there any reason why I can't do it right now?

ALICE

Me too.

PAUL

Of course you can. Marie?

MARIE

Want us to hold hands?

MARIE takes the hand of DENISE and ALICE and they join hands with PAUL. BOB watches silently.

PAUL

Lord Jesus. Thank you for dying on the cross for us. We know we are sinners. We confess those things in our lives that aren't pleasing to you. Forgive us and cleanse us. Right now we ask that you walk into the open door of our hearts. We trust you as our Savior. Take over control of our lives; make us each the type of person that you created us to be. In Christ's name. Amen.

LIGHTS FADE OUT.

<u>SONG</u>

MESSAGE - Pastor

Scene 10

LIGHTS COME UP.

PAUL is working on the fireplace and MARIE is making some notes at the front desk. BOB, DENISE, and ALICE enter.

MARIE

Good morning Bob...Denise. The Highway Patrol has cleared the road for travel. You gonna finish that drive up to Handale?

DENISE

Yes, we almost hate to go. We're so glad we got stuck here.

MARIE

Well your coming here was an answer to prayer.

DENISE

Before we check out, Bob has some wonderful news.

BOB

Last night, after I went to bed, I couldn't sleep. I kept thinking I need to do this. I need to do this right now. So I did the simple thing you suggested. I said 'Yes' to God. Then because it was such a quiet, interior thing. I felt I should tell someone, so I woke up Denise, and I told her, "Well, I'm a Christian now."

DENISE

And I said, "Do you feel any different?"

PAUL

Did you?

BOB

Well...no flashes of lightning or anything...but I felt a special sense of..quiet.

DENISE

Isn't that great? This is the best Christmas that we've ever had.

MARIE

Well, this certainly calls for a celebration.

PAUL

Here, here. A round of eggnog for everyone.

PAUL and MARIE pass out the glasses.

Here's to Bob...Denise...and Alice, you've made this a special Christmas for all of us. And here's to your new life...

MARIE

...and remember...He's the reason for the Season.

ALICE

...and to all a MERRY CHRISTMAS!

ALL

Here, here.

LIGHTS FADE OUT.

<u>SONG</u>

Leave It To Otter

By Skip Martin

PRELUDE

SONG

Scene 1

LIGHTS COME UP to reveal the foyer to the Weaver residence.

BARBARA WEAVER ENTERS holding two lunch boxes.

BARBARA

Billy....Otter...you boys better hurry or you'll be late for school.

BILLY
(From offstage)

Coming mom.

OTTER
(From offstage)

Coming mom.

BILLY ENTERS rushing down the stairs. He quickly grabs his lunchbox from BARBARA and heads to the door.

BILLY

Bye mom.

BARBARA

Billy?

BILLY

Yes, ma'am?

BARBARA

You haven't forgotten that you drew Mary Ann's name for the class gift exchange, have you?

BILLY

Gee no mom. How could a guy forget something like that?

BARBARA

Well...have you decided what Christmas gift you'd like to get her yet?

BILLY

Gee, mom. I don't know what kind of stuff to get for a girl. *(Pauses)* Is she too old for a doll?

BARBARA

Yes. I think so. Would you like me to pick something out for you to give her?

BILLY

Gee, Mom. Would you? That would be great. Bye, Mom.

BARBARA

Goodbye dear. Have a good day. *(Pauses)* Ot.t.t..e..e..r.

BILLY EXITS. OTTER ENTERS rushing down the stairs.

OTTER

Bye mom.

OTTER takes his lunchbox from BARBARA and heads to the door.

BARBARA

Wait a minute young man. What is that...thing in your back pocket?

OTTER

(Reaches into back pocket and pulls out toy alligator)

Oh...this. I'm taking it in to show Mrs. Clement. She says we should bring something to class for show and tell.

BARBARA

An alligator?

OTTER

Yeah. Isn't he neat? I think Mrs. Clement will really like him.

BARBARA

Oh...I'm sure she will. Um..Otter you might want to warn her that it's not real before you bring it out to show to her.

OTTER

Gee...mom. Do really think that would scare her?

BARBARA

He's very frightening. Take it from you mother.

OTTER

(Starts waving alligator toy around)

Grr.r.r.r..w.w.w.l.

BARBARA

(Sternly)

Ot..t..t.er. You put that away and remember what I said.

OTTER

(Putting toy back in pocket)

Yes ma'am.

BARBARA

Bye dear. And don't forget to give that note I gave you to Mrs. Clement.

OTTER

No ma'am. I won't. Bye mom.

BARBARA

Goodbye dear.

OTTER EXITS.

BARBARA

I hope that boy doesn't lose that note...again.

LIGHTS FADE OUT.

<u>SONG</u>

Scene 2

LIGHTS COME UP to reveal OTTER standing in the school hallway closely examining an envelope. BECKY ENTERS.

BECKY

Otter. What ya doin?

OTTER

Lookin.

BECKY

What'cha lookin at?

OTTER

This note Mrs. Clement gave me to take home to my parents.

BECKY

(Worried)

Mrs. Clement gave you a note to take home to your parents?

OTTER

(Holding envelope up to ceiling trying to read note inside)

Yup.

BECKY

What's it say?

OTTER

Don't know. I can't read it.

BECKY

It can't be good.

OTTER

Can't?

BECKY

Nope. It's never good when the teacher sends a note home to your parents.

OTTER

It's not?

BECKY
(Shakes head)

Nope. What'd you do?

OTTER

I don't know. I can't remember. I didn't get yelled at for anything.

BECKY

You must have done something.

OTTER
(Shrugs)

BECKY

Maybe it's for standing on your chair?

OTTER

Nah. I already got in trouble for that.

BECKY

Did you throw any spitballs at anybody?

OTTER

I don't think so. I already got in trouble for that too.

BECKY

Did you pull Kathy's pigtails again?

OTTER
(Thinking)

No.o.o.. I haven't done that in a long time. (Pauses) I don't know what I did.

BECKY

Boy, Otter. I'm glad I'm not in your shoes. You're always getting in trouble. I'll bet ya that when your parents get that note, you'll get in so much trouble that you won't get any Christmas presents or anything. See ya.

OTTER

Yeah. See ya, Becky.

BECKY EXITS.

OTTER holds up envelope one more time, trying to read its contents, but then gives up. He stuffs the envelope loosely in his sweater pocket, and begins to head off stage.

OTTER

I sure hope I don't get in trouble again. I was already in trouble two times last week.

LIGHTS FADE OUT.

SONG

Scene 3

LIGHTS COME UP to reveal the bedroom of BILLY and OTTER.

BILLY
(Shaking head)

Boy, Otter. You really know how to mess things up. Ya just got clobbered last week. What'da you do this time?

OTTER

Nothin. Honest Billy. I didn't do anything.

BILLY

Well....then why did you get the note?

OTTER

I dunno.

BILLY

Let me see it.

OTTER

Okay. (*reaches into sweater pocket to get note. When he realizes its not there, he searches the other sweater pocket and then his pants pockets, becoming more anxious as he realizes that he no longer has the note.)* I can't find it.

BILLY

What'd' ya mean you can't find it? Didn't you just get the note today?

OTTER

I put it right here in my pocket. I'm sure I did. I was talking with Becky and right after I talked to her I put the note right here. And now its gone.

BILLY

You sure you didn't take it out and put it somewhere?

OTTER

Nope. I didn't take it out or 'nothin. I came straight home.

BILLY

Boy, Otter. Now you're really gonna get it. When your teacher finds out you lost the note she's gonna think you did it on purpose. Then she's really gonna be sore at you.

OTTER

Honest, Billy. I didn't lose it on purpose. It was an accident.

BILLY

Well....if I was you I would think up a really good excuse or you're liable to get grounded for the whole 5th grade.

OTTER

Gee, Billy do you really think so?

BILLY

Yeah, I think so. And you know that new Flexible Flyer sled you wanted?

OTTER

Yeah.

BILLY

You can forget about it.

OTTER

(In dejection)

Ohhhh, no. What should I say?

BILLY

Oh, no. I'm not getting mixed up in this. I'm always getting in trouble for your messes.

OTTER

Please Billy. I couldn't think up an excuse that good by myself. Please? Would you help me? If I get the sled...I'll let you use it for a whole month.

BILLY

Oh...All right but I'm probably going to be sorry.

BARBARA

(From offstage)

Boys, wash up. It's time for dinner.

BILLY and OTTER

Ok. Mom.

BILLY

We'll be there in just a minute.

OTTER

What should I do?

BILLY

Maybe we can make up another note?

OTTER

You mean we can just make a note pretending to be Mrs. Clement?

BILLY

Yeah. That's what I mean.

OTTER

Well...what would the note say?

BILLY

Well...it could say that you did something stupid and that Mom and Dad should punish you.

OTTER

I dunno Billy. That doesn't sound so good.

BILLY

Well its gotta sound realistic.

OTTER

Yeah, I guess so...

BILLY

Listen, Otter. We gotta go to dinner. We'll make the note after we're done.

OTTER

I sure hope Mom doesn't ask me about the note I was supposed to give Mrs. Clement.

BILLY

Why?

OTTER

'Cause I lost that note too.

BILLY

(Shakes head)

Boy, Otter you sure know how to make a mess.

LIGHTS FADE OUT.

<u>SONG</u>

<u>SONG</u>

Scene 4

LIGHTS COME UP to reveal the Weaver dining room. The Weaver family is seated around the table eating dinner.

BARBARA

Well...boys. How did school go today?

OTTER and BILLY look nervously at each other.

BILLY

Uh...everything was fine Mom.

OTTER

Uh...yeah everything was fine Mom.

BARBARA

(Sensing that boys are acting a bit strange)

Well..I'm...I'm glad to hear that. Billy did anything special happen at your school?

BILLY

Uh...oh...no Mom. Nothing special. Um...everything was just fine.

BARBARA

Yes. I can see that. How about you Otter? Anything special happen at your school?

OTTER

Uh..no ma'am. Nothing special. Um...everything went swell.

BARBARA

(Not quite buying it)

Oh. I see.

HUGH

Well...um...Otter. I'm glad to hear everything was so....swell

BARBARA

Otter, did Mrs. Clement say anything about the note?

OTTER

The note?

BARBARA

Yes. The note. The note I gave you this morning to give to Mrs. Clement.

OTTER

O.o.o.oh. That note.

OTTER hesitates.

HUGH

Yes. Otter, that note. Your mother wants to know if Mrs. Clement got the note she sent you to school with.

OTTER

Well...I gave it to her all right...but she couldn't read it on account of the accident.

BARBARA

An accident? What kind of accident?

OTTER

Oh. It was just a small one. Wally Hild just broke his leg. But he's okay.

BARBARA

Broke his leg!

HUGH

He's okay? Well...I'll have to call Fred and find out how the boy's doing.

OTTER

Oh...I wouldn't do that.

HUGH

Why not?

OTTER

On account tha.... that Wally's grandmother died. They're sort of in mourning.

HUGH

(Suspiciously)

I see. Well this must have all happened quite recently. I was speaking to Fred at the office today and he didn't mention anything about it all

OTTER

Oh...uh...I think it's the secret grandmother that they don't want anyone to know about.

BARBARA

Well...I certainly don't know anything about a secret grandmother

OTTER

Oh...that's because it's a secret.

HUGH

Now listen Otter, this had better not be one of your cockamaney stories. You know how your mother and I feel about lying.

OTTER

Oh, no sir. Uh...may I be excused? I have some homework to do.

BARBARA

You're doing homework without having to be reminded?

OTTER

Yes, ma'am.

BILLY

May I be excused too?

HUGH

I suppose you have some homework to do too?

BILLY

Um. Yes, sir.

HUGH

Yes, boys you may be excused...but I expect you to be doing some homework.

OTTER and BILLY

Yes, sir.

OTTER and BILLY EXIT.

BARBARA

Hugh, I don't like this. What do you suppose the boys are up to?

HUGH

I don't know, but we better find out before somebody else dies.

LIGHTS FADE OUT.

<u>SONG</u>

Scene 5

LIGHTS COME UP to reveal BARBARA sitting on the living room sofa knitting a sweater After a moment, HUGH ENTERS.

HUGH

Well...I just got off the phone with Fred. Both his mother and Ethel's mother are perfectly fine. They haven't had a death in the family for years.

BARBARA

Oh, Hugh. Where do you suppose that story the boys told came from?

HUGH

(Angrily)

I don't know. But I plan on finding out. I simply cannot tolerate lying.

BARBARA

Are you going to talk to the boys?

HUGH

As soon as I develop the best strategy. Can't let those boys get the drop on me.

BARBARA

Get the drop on you?

HUGH

It's an old gun fighting expression....never mind dear. You just need to let them know who's boss...that's all.

BARBARA

Hugh...this isn't a gunfight or a....a boxing match. These are just boys. Maybe they didn't tell us the truth because they are afraid of us.

HUGH

Afraid of us? Why on earth would they be afraid of us? Dear...if I've told them once, I've told them a dozen times that they can always come to me whenever they have a problem. But I simply will not tolerate lying. Do you know what Fred told me? He said that his son Wally hasn't had a broken bone in his life. As a matter of fact, he just came home from the church softball game. Seems that Wally hit the game winning home run.

BARBARA

Oh, Hugh.

HUGH

Well...if they're going to lie to their father....

BARBARA

....and Mother...

HUGH

...and Mother. We're just going to have to make them wish they never had.

BARBARA

Dear, if they weren't afraid of you, maybe they would feel brave enough to tell the truth?

HUGH

But why should they be afraid of me? I'm their father.

BARBARA

Well if I was a little boy and you came to talk to me like that I would be afraid of you.

HUGH

Well what do you expect me to do? March on up there and give them a pat on the back for lying?

BARBARA

No. But you can make sure that the first thing they understand is that you are a loving father.

HUGH

Maybe you're right. My Dad was pretty tough, but I always understood that he loved me. Before he would give me a switching he would roll up his sleeves and say, "This is going to hurt me as much as it hurts you". I didn't believe him then, but maybe I understand it a little more now.

BARBARA

Dear, you never told me that your father used corporal punishment.

HUGH

Well dear...it's not the kind of thing you tell your sweetheart when you're trying to make a good impression.

BARBARA

Is there anything else you haven't told me?

HUGH

(Chuckling)

Well there was the time when...uh...never mind. Seems like they have a manual on everything else. Why don't they have one on boys?

BARBARA

They do dear, it's all in a book called love.

LIGHTS FADE OUT.

<u>SONG</u>

Scene 6

LIGHTS COME UP to reveal OTTER and BILLY in their bedroom seated at their desk.

OTTER

Gee, Billy, do you think they went for it?

BILLY

I don't think so.

OTTER

Yeah. I don't think so either. Well...what are we going to do now?

BILLY

I don't know Otter, but why did you have to come up with that story about Wally and his grandmother? When Mom and Dad find out they're gonna hit the ceiling.

OTTER

How do you know they're going to find out?

BILLY

They'll find out. They always find out.

OTTER

Yeah. How do they do that?

BILLY

I dunno. I guess that's their job. They're parents.

OTTER

Yeah...I guess you're right.

There is a KNOCK on the door.

HUGH

(From offstage)

Boys, I want to speak with you for a minute.

BILLY

Yes, Dad.

HUGH ENTERS.

HUGH

Boys, your Mother and I have had a talk about some things that have been going on around here and uh...we need to see that it gets straightened out. You see I spoke to Fred on the telephone just a little while ago. Otter do you have something you want to tell me?

OTTER

Yes, Dad. I guess I told a story I shouldn't have.

HUGH

That's right, Otter you told a lie. Wally's grandmother didn't die did she?

OTTER

No sir.

HUGH

Do you want to explain to me why you told that lie to your mother and I?

OTTER

(Rapidly)

Well....it was all on account that I lost that note Mom sent me to school with and she told me not to lose it and I did so I didn't want to get in trouble 'cause I already got in trouble twice last week and I didn't want to lose my Christmas presents.

HUGH

I see...well I hope you realize that telling a lie well usually only make matters worse. Once you lie to someone, and they find out, they'll learn not to trust you anymore. Pretty soon lots of people won't trust you and then where will you be? Otter...your reputation is one of the most important things you have. You don't want to ruin it do you?

OTTER

No, sir.

HUGH

Well...its my job to raise you properly and to provide the appropriate discipline when warranted.

OTTER

You mean punishment?

HUGH

Yes, son. That's exactly what I mean. What do you think an appropriate punishment would be for your actions this evening?

OTTER

Gee, Dad, you mean I have to decide my own punishment?

HUGH

Well son, as part of learning how to do the right thing, I think that would be appropriate. Your mother and I will take your recommendation into consideration.

OTTER

Yes, Dad.

HUGH

How much time do you think you'll need to uh...come up with your recommendation?

OTTER

I dunno...can I have 'til tomorrow or how 'bout the day after tomorrow?

HUGH

All right son.....that will....that will be fine. I hope our talk has helped you learn how important it is to always tell the truth.

OTTER

Yes, Dad.

HUGH turns to leave and heads toward the door.

OTTER

Dad, can I ask you a question?

HUGH

Sure son, what is it?

OTTER

Supposin' you had a friend that was always gettin' in trouble. And supposin' he wanted to do the right things but somehow he ended up doing the wrong things so he kept gettin' in trouble. But he really wanted to do the right things... who could a fellow like that talk to to help him stop doing the wrong thing and start doing the right thing

HUGH

...and this is a friend of yours?

OTTER

(Nods head)

HUGH

Hmn. That's a very interesting question, son. *(Pauses)* Well...I suppose that if I had a friend like that I would recommend that he go down and talk to Pastor Bob. Perhaps he would have a good suggestion on how this fellow might get things turned around.

OTTER

The pastor, huh?

HUGH

Yes...I think that might be worth a try.

OTTER

Okay. Thanks dad.

HUGH

All right, well I'm glad we had this talk, now...uh...finish your homework and get ready for bed. We'll decide on how to handle this day after tomorrow, all right?

OTTER and BILLY

Yes, sir.

HUGH EXITS.

BILLY

Boy, Otter, you sure do know how to get into messes. What are you gonna do now? If you come up with a punishment that's too soft, they're liable to really give it to ya and if you come up with a punishment that's too tough, they might make you do it.

OTTER

Yeah.

BILLY

So what are you gonna do?

OTTER

Don't know. But I do know one thing?

BILLY

What's that?

OTTER

I'm gonna talk to Pastor Bob.

LIGHTS FADE OUT.

<u>SONG</u>

Scene 7

LIGHTS COME UP to reveal OTTER seated in PASTOR BOB'S study.

PASTOR BOB

Well young man to what can I attribute the honor of seeing you this afternoon? Ms. Carol said it was a very urgent matter.

OTTER

Yes, sir. You see...I have a friend who always gets in trouble.

PASTOR BOB

I see.

OTTER

He doesn't mean to. He tries to do the right thing, but somehow he always ends up doing something wrong.

PASTOR BOB

Yes. Go on.

OTTER

So I....uh my friend....would like to know how he can stop doing the wrong things all the time?

PASTOR BOB

Well...Timothy...

OTTER

...all my friends call me Otter.

PASTOR BOB

All right Otter. Let me tell you about a friend I have. What's interesting about my friend is that He gives me exactly the kind of help that you would like your friend to have.

OTTER

He does?

PASTOR BOB

Yes, as a matter of fact He was born to be a helper.

OTTER

Gee...I didn't know a person could be born to do something like that.

PASTOR BOB

Well...this friend...is not just an ordinary fellow. You see....although He was a man, He's also God's son. And God sent Him into this world to live with us just so that He could help people stop doing the wrong things and start doing the right things.

OTTER

You mean just like I want to...er...I mean my friend wants to?

PASTOR BOB

That's right Otter. You see son, your friend is not the only one with that particular problem. Every one us deals with it to some degree or another. That's exactly why God sent my friend, His Son, to help us all out.

OTTER

Gee Pastor Bob...I never thought that other people have trouble doing the wrong things too.

PASTOR BOB

Of course they do, son. We all do. Even me.

OTTER

Well...if everyone has trouble doing the right things...how does God's son help all of them?

PASTOR BOB

Well He has a helper. And that helper is called the Holy Spirit. And anyone who trusts in God's Son...whose name is Jesus, by the way...will receive the Holy Spirit as a helper. So whenever they have trouble deciding whether they are doing the right thing or the wrong thing, the Holy Spirit will be able to help them.

OTTER

That's it! That's what I need.

PASTOR BOB

Don't you mean that's what your *friend* needs?

OTTER

No....no...there really isn't a friend. I mean I have lots of friends, but that wasn't really a friend I was talking about. It was me.

PASTOR BOB

Well...Otter...I have a confession to make too. I knew that from the very beginning of our conversation.

OTTER

Gee Pastor Bob, how did you know that?

PASTOR BOB

(Smiling)

Let's just say I had a little help from a friend.

OTTER

(Thinking)

O.h.h....

PASTOR BOB

Otter, let me explain. God's Son, Jesus, was sent to us by God to teach us about Him, to help us understand what God is like, and to take our punishment for all of the things we've done wrong in our lives. He did that by dying on a Cross. But after His death, God raised Him up and made Him alive again. The Bible tells us that everyone who believes and trusts in Jesus, accepting God's gift of His punishment in the place of our own, will receive forgiveness from God for all the things they've done wrong in their lives. The best part is, that they will then be given a place with God in heaven.

OTTER

And the Holy Spirit will help them too?

PASTOR BOB

(Chuckling)

Yes, the Holy Spirit will help them too. Otter here's what I want you to do. Think about what I've said. Tonight when you say your prayers...say a simple little prayer. Tell God that you want to stop doing things that are wrong, ask Him to forgive you for the things you've already done wrong, and thank Him for sending Jesus into this world to take your punishment as His own. Then tell Him you want to start a new life and to send His helper, the Holy Spirit into your life. That's all you have to do. Then you just trust Him, God will do the rest.

OTTER

Gee, Pastor Bob, that's all I have to do. It's that easy?

PASTOR BOB

Otter...it's that easy. You just make the decision first in your heart, God will understand your words and handle it all from there.

OTTER

(Getting up to leave)

Thanks Pastor Bob. I'm gonna try it. I sure hope this works.

PASTOR BOB

Tell you what Otter, I'll say a little prayer myself tonight just for you...just to make sure it does.

OTTER

(Shakes Pastor's hand)

Gee, thanks Pastor Bob. You're swell.

PASTOR BOB

Well thank you Otter. That's the best compliment I've had all day.

LIGHTS FADE OUT.

<u>SONG</u>

Scene 8

LIGHTS COME UP to reveal OTTER who is straightening up his room. HUGH KNOCKS on the door and then enters.

HUGH

Well Otter...straightening up your room I see.

OTTER

Yes, sir.

HUGH

Well son, I...uh...thought this might be a good time to finish our talk. The one we had the other day?

OTTER

Yes sir.

HUGH

Have you given some thought to what we talked about?

OTTER

Yes, sir.

HUGH

And have you decided on a fair punishment for the things you did.?

OTTER

(Nervously)

Um. Yes, sir.

HUGH

All right. Well...uh..son....why don't you share it with me then.

OTTER

Well....I told those lies 'cause I was afraid of losing my Christmas presents. So... as punishment.....(quickly) I should have to give up all my presents.

HUGH

(Incredulously)

You would give up all your Christmas presents as punishment? *(Pauses)* Otter, your mother and I would never take away your Christmas presents in order to punish you.

OTTER

You wouldn't?

HUGH

No. Of course not. What on earth ever gave you that idea?

OTTER

I dunno. I guess I listened to someone at school.

HUGH

Otter, when your mother and I discipline you...we don't do it to be mean or spiteful...we do it because we love you and we want you to grow up to be a fine young man. Do you understand that?

OTTER

Yeah...I think so.

HUGH

We were upset that you lost the note because it shows irresponsibility. Being responsible is an important part of growing up. And do you understand now that trying to cover it up with a lie will only make matters worse?

OTTER

I do now. It won't ever happen again.

HUGH

Well...doing the right thing won't always be easy. Sometimes the temptation will come for you to do it again.

OTTER

I know, but now I can stop temp'tion 'cause I have a new friend.

HUGH

You do?

OTTER

Yes, sir. Pastor Bob told me 'bout Jesus and the Holy Spirit, and how if I ask Him for help, He'll be my friend and help me make the right choice..

HUGH

Pastor Bob said that did he? Well...he's a very wise man. Tell you what, Otter. I think you've learned your lesson. So...I think this whole experience has been punishment enough for you. Let's chalk this one up to a learning experience.... and uh...make sure that it doesn't happen again.

OTTER

You mean I won't lose my Christmas presents or nothin'?

HUGH

(Chuckling)

No. You won't lose your Christmas presents or anything.

OTTER

Gee Dad, you're swell.

HUGH

(Hugs Otter)

We'll thank you Otter. You're...uh...pretty swell yourself.

LIGHTS FADE OUT.

<u>SONG</u>

Scene 9

LIGHTS COME UP to reveal the living room of the Weaver residence. After a few moments the telephone rings. BARBARA ENTERS and walks over to the phone.

BARBARA

Hello. Why hello Mrs. Clement. I'm so glad you returned my call. Uh..huh. Yes...uh...huh. Well....it doesn't surprise me. It seems that using the Otter as a note courier is not the best idea. Well after he lost the last note I sent you so I wanted to make sure we talked. *(Pause)* No....no. I'll talk to him about it tonight. Don't worry about a thing. I'm sure he'll be very excited. *(Pause)* Oh, of course, we'll certainly be there. Thank you for calling. Goodbye.

HUGH enters, intently looking at the newspaper he is carrying..

BARBARA

Hugh?

HUGH

(Reading paper)

Yes, dear.

BARBARA

That was Mrs. Clement I was just talking to on the phone. Apparently when she didn't get the note I sent her, she sent a note home with The Otter. She was concerned that she hadn't heard back from me.

HUGH

(Still reading paper)

(Puts down paper) Let me guess. He lost Mrs. Clement's note too.

BARBARA

Apparently, so. Well...we just got it all straightened out. I think I'll talk to The Otter about it right now.

HUGH

(Reading paper again)

Sounds like a good idea.

BARBARA

OTTER. Would you come down here for a minute? I need to talk to you about something.

OTTER

(From offstage)

Coming mom!

OTTER hurries in from offstage.

BARBARA

Otter...you know that note Mrs. Clement sent you home with?

OTTER

What note?

HUGH

(Puts down paper)

Otter! *(Raising tone of voice)*.

OTTER

OOOH. THAT note.

HUGH and BARBARA

Yes. THAT note.

BARBARA

I just got off the phone with Mrs. Clement. She thinks you must have lost it.

OTTER

But I didn't do nuthin' wrong. Honest, I didn't. I didn't chew any gum, or throw any spitballs, or pull any pigtails or nothin'.

BARBARA

Otter, Mrs. Clement didn't send the note home because you did something wrong.

OTTER

She didn't?

BARBARA

No. In fact, she said you've become one of her best students.

OTTER

She did?

BARBARA

Yes. So she has decided that you should be honored by having a special part in the school Christmas play.

OTTER

I am?

BARBARA

Isn't that wonderful?

OTTER

Yeah. I guess so. What's the special part?

BARBARA

You'll be one of the three kings. Isn't that wonderful?

OTTER

Gee, mom. Won't I have to wear a fancy costume?

HUGH

Well...you won't be able to wear jeans and a tee shirt.

BILLY enters carrying a shopping bag.

BILLY

Oh, uh....Hi Mom, hi Dad.

HUGH

Hello, son. What took you so long? Didn't you say that you were just stopping by Eddie's house for minute?

BILLY

Yeah. But....well...I decided that it wasn't fair for Mom to have to get my present for the class gift exchange, so I figured out something that I could get that even a girl would like.

HUGH

(Mischievously)

That's not easy to do

BARBARA

(Reproachfully) Hugh. *(Turning to Billy)* William that was very nice of you. What did you decide to get her?

BILLY

Well jeepers Mom, everybody loves Elvis Presley. So I decided to get her this new 45 record. It's got this new song all the kids like called....uh... "Hound Dog".

HUGH

Son...are you sure she's going like a song about a hound...dog?

BARBARA

William, I'm sure she'll appreciate it very much.

BILLY

Thanks, mom.

HUGH

Well, Otter, I'm sure Mrs. Clement would like to know as soon as possible whether you'll accept that part in the Christmas play.

OTTER

Dad?

HUGH

Yes, son.

OTTER

Do I have to take her another note?

HUGH

(Chuckling)

No, son. You don't have to take another note. Your mother will give Mrs. Clement a call tomorrow.

OTTER

Well...okay. Then...I guess I can do the part.

HUGH

Well it seems like we should do something special. Whad'ya say we head down to Dan's Malt Shop to celebrate.

OTTER

Can we? That would be swell.

BILLY

Yeah. Okay, Dad.

BARBARA

I'd love to.

HUGH

Well..then let's go.

ALL start heading to the door.

BARBARA

Otter...the school picture we ordered last month hasn't come home yet. You did give Mrs. Clement the money I sent you to school with....didn't you?

OTTER

Mom...Dad...I just remembered I have homework to do. You guys can go without me. See ya.

OTTER runs back into the house and up the stairs.

BARBARA

OTT..E.E.R.

HUGH

OTTER.

BARBARA

Hugh, I'm worried about The Otter.

HUGH

Don't worry about a thing dear. The answers are all in a book called Love.

LIGHTS FADE OUT.

MESSAGE

<u>SONG</u>

Please see the [illegible] and application at the end of [illegible] availability [illegible] of application [illegible] Skip Martin, 1820 Main Street, Suite One, [illegible] Florida [illegible], or www.christmasplays[illegible]

A Very "Jobial" Christmas

By Skip Martin

SONG

Scene 1

LIGHTS COME UP.

EMMA is seated in the living room of the BERNDT family home, which is modestly decorated with sofa, coffee table and recliner. There is a phone on a stand near the sofa. Behind the furniture rests a very large Christmas Tree. EMMA is intently engaged with her laptop computer. LOUISE ENTERS carrying a bag with a scrapbook and scrapbooking materials.

LOUISE

Ok, Emma, I'm leaving.

EMMA

Uh huh.

LOUISE

I'm going to be gone for scrapbooking the whole day.

EMMA

Uh huh.

LOUISE

(Pointedly trying to get her attention)

You can reach me on my cell phone.

EMMA

Uh huh.

LOUISE

Emma, have you heard a word I've said?

EMMA

(Looking up)

What? Oh...I'm sorry Mom. I was um...facebooking Megan.

LOUSE

Honestly, Emma, sometimes I think you're just a little two addicted to Facebook.

EMMA

No way, Mom. I haven't talked to my friends in a whole day! I'm just trying to set up a lunch date with all of my friends. I haven't seen anyone since I got home.

LOUISE

Well...you're not going to be here very long, you should probably plan a little time together with your Mom and Dad too?

EMMA

I know. I KNOW.

LOUISE

Have you told your Dad yet?

EMMA

You mean about spending Christmas with Jason's family?

LOUISE

Yes.

EMMA

No. Not yet.

LOUISE

He is sure to be disappointed. Y'know, with you just getting home from college.

EMMA

Yeah. I know. But I don't know how to tell him.

LOUISE

Well...putting it off isn't going to help. You better tell him pretty soon.

EMMA

I know.

JEB ENTERS. He is carrying a Blackberry, which commands his compete attention as he slowly walks into the scene.

LOUSE

Have you done all of your Christmas shopping?

EMMA

Almost. But I don't know what to get Dad? He's so hard to shop for. I mean... if he wants something, he just goes out and gets it.

JEB realizes that the two women are talking about him. He lowers the hand holding the Blackberry, and steps back to the side of the Christmas Tree, attempting to conceal himself from their view.

LOUISE

Well I got him a Kindle...like we discussed. Maybe you can get him some books to go with it?

EMMA

MOM! You bought him a Kindle! I can't believe you did that. He specifically said he wanted an iPad.

LOUISE

Well aren't they basically the same thing? Anyway, I saw the Kindle on sale at Target, so I decided to get it.

EMMA

O...kaaay. But he did want an iPad. I mean it's got some features on it that he really liked.

LOUISE

Well the salesman told me it was just as good. Anyways, I have to go. I've been planning this scrapbooking session for months.

EMMA

(Putting away laptop)

Wait...hold on...I'll head out with you. I'm going to Megan's.

EMMA AND LOUISE head offstage.

LOUISE

(Hugging EMMA)

I can hardly believe my daughter's home for Christmas break.

JEB steps out from behind the Tree and heads downstage center.

JEB

A Kindle!...she's getting me a Kindle? I told her I wanted an iPad. I even told her...it's got the color screen, it's got the Web browser, you can use it for Facebook. I can't believe she's getting a Kindle, *(JEB is interrupted by the buzzer on his Blackberry)* Hello? Oh..yes, Tom.. Uh..huh. Really? No...no. I'll get on it right away. I know...oh, I KNOW...it's our biggest account. Don't worry, DON'T WORRY. Look... tell him that I'm heading over to meet him right away. In fact, I'm on my way right now. *(Pauses)* Got it. *(Hangs up).* Arrgh. I can't believe this is happening on the biggest account we have.

JEB grabs his jacket and starts heading offstage.

JEB

A Kindle?

JEB EXITS.

LIGHTS FADE OUT.

<u>SONG</u>

Scene 2

LIGHTS COME UP.

Once again showing the BERNDT living room.

JEB ENTERS. He looks like he's been walking ten miles, even though it may have only been three or four. JEB briefly looks around until he finds what he is looking for, his briefcase. JEB takes the case over to the couch, then sits down and opens it up.

JEB

Ah. Found it! Can't believe I left this at home.

The TELEPHONE RINGS. JEB puts down his briefcase and gets up to answer it.

JEB

Hello? Oh, hi Louise. You won't believe what happened to me. My car broke down. Yeah...Tom called me about y'know that really big account I have and the client was having a problem so I told him I would go meet with the client right away....and so I'm on the way and my stinkin' car breaks down. No...it won't crank or anything. Just came to a complete stop. All I could do was pull it over to the side of the road. I was gonna call AAA, but then I realized I didn't have the client file, so I decided to walk back home. *(Pauses)* What? You're kidding! Your brother's at the airport? Well...it's certainly nice to get some warning. Great...just great. *(Pause)* No...no...it's not that. I like them, really I do. It's just that y'now...they're religious nuts, that's all. *(Pauses)* Look...I just don't want to hear about Jesus all the time at Christmas, OK..Well, obviously, I can't pick them up. My car is temporarily indisposed. *(Pauses)* All right, I'll do what I can to clean the place up.

JEB hangs up the phone.

JEB

Great.....just great. The brother and sister-in-law visiting are the last thing I need right now. *(Takes a deep breath)* Ok, ok, I better call that client. (*Reaches into his pocket for his Blackberry but realizes with a shock that it's not there)* Where'd I put my Blackberry?

JEB goes to his briefcase to look there and then with increasingly frantic movements, looks throughout the living room without success.

JEB

(Sits down to think)

Where'd I put my Blackberry?

JEB

(Jumping up)

The car! I left it in the car! Ok, ok, better call the client. *(Pauses)* SHEE-OOOT. OH, GREAT! Just.....great. The number is in the Blackberry. ARGH! I don't want to walk back to the car.

JEB trudges over to pick up the briefcase and heads offstage.

LIGHTS FADE OUT.

<u>SONG</u>

Scene 3

LIGHTS COME UP.

JEB ENTERS. He looks worse than he did before. He puts the briefcase down and plops down on the couch to catch his breath.

JEB

If I ever catch that son-of-a-gun I'm gonna kill him. No, I'm not just going to kill him. I'm going to take his scrawny little neck and I'm going to twist it into..... a new type of pretzel.

EMMA ENTERS carrying some luggage.

EMMA

Dad....you don't sound yourself today.

JEB

You wouldn't be yourself either if someone stole your iPhone.

EMMA

You have an iPhone?

JEB

(Dripping sarcasm)

No. I don't have an iPhone. I was just trying to....Never mind. As you know, I have a Blackberry. Well...I was on my way to meet a client, when my car broke down. I came back home, and then I realized that I had left my Blackberry in the car. So....then I went back to the car to get it and that's when I found out that some nice person decided to steal it.

EMMA

Ohhhh. That's awful.

JEB

Yes, it is. And not only that, my client's phone number is on it and I don't have the phone number any other place. I would try calling Tom, my boss, but he's on an airplane somewhere right now. So it looks like I have just lost the largest account I have. Merry Christmas.

EMMA

I'm so sorry Dad.

JEB

Well it's certainly not your fault. Hey, what are the bags for?

EMMA

These bags?

JEB

Yes, those bags. I think those bags are the only bags in this room..

EMMA

Dad...um... why don't you have a seat?

JEB hesitates.

JEB

Why?

EMMA waits while JEB sits down.

EMMA

You see, I told Mom, but I was afraid to tell you, because I didn't want you to get upset.

JEB

I'm already upset.

EMMA

Dad, please. You're making this harder. See...Jason and his family have invited me to spend Christmas with them. And...I really like him...and so I would like to meet his family....and so I said yes.

JEB

Ahhh. I see. So you're going to go spend Christmas with um....Jason's family in uh...Atlanta. And so that's why....the bags....

EMMA

I wanted to tell you before....but I knew you would be hurt.

JEB

Sure.

EMMA

So...anyways...I've gotta go or I'll miss my flight.

JEB

No...no. You go ahead. I'll be fine.

EMMA

You sure?

JEB

Yes, I'm sure. Besides the Big Game will be on in a little while. I won't be aware of another thing in this world.

EMMA

Ok. Dad. Well....I love you.

JEB

Give my regards to Jason...

EMMA

I will...

JEB

....and the family.

EMMA

OK.

EMMA EXITS.

JEB

(Wistfully)

I've never spent a single Christmas without that girl. *(Pauses)* Merry Christmas.

LIGHTS FADE OUT.

<u>SONG</u>

Scene 4

LIGHTS COME UP.

JEB ENTERS carrying a large soft drink and a bag of chips. He sets them down on the coffee table, plops down on the couch, and picks up the remote.

JEB

(Rubbing his hands together)

All right. Now... I am ready for THE GAME! *(Chuckles to himself)*

THE HOME TELEPHONE RINGS.

JEB

(Groans)

NOW what? Don't people have enough sense not to call at a time like this. For crying out loud!

JEB rises and walks to the phone.

JEB

Hello? *(Pauses)* Tom? Yeah, I know. Listen, it's a long story but I left my Blackberry in the car and someone apparently has stolen it. By the way, aren't you on the way to California? Ahh...switching planes. *(Pauses)* Mr. Hardcastle called you? Yeah....well I tried to call him back but the number was on my Blackberry, which is where I keep everything. *(Pauses)* But....but...he can't do that....we have a contract. *(Pauses)* Listen, OK...Tom....calm down, CALM DOWN! I KNOW it's our biggest account. Listen I'm sure he'll calm down once I get a chance to talk to him...Tom? Hello? Tom? Are you there, TOM? Great, just great. Looks like I lost him.

JEB walks over and plops down on the couch again.

JEB

Am I having a bad day or what? I mean what have I done to deserve all this? Geez! All right....forget it...forget it...forget all about it. It's time for some football.

JEB picks up the remote and presses the button. He waits a moment and tries again. After nothing happens a second time he gets up and walks over to the set. He tries pushing the power button and steps back.

JEB

(Standing by set)

Hmmmmm. Is this thing plugged in? *(Looks at plug and confirms that its plugged in)*

What could be wrong with this thing? *(After examining further JEB realizes that the bulb is out)* Oh, for crying out loud it looks like the projection bulb is out. *(He yells at TV)* You could have gone out any time, any time at all, in the last three years, but NOOO, you have to choose the day of the biggest game of the year. *(Sighs)* Great, just great. MERRY Christmas.

LIGHTS FADE OUT.

<u>SONG</u>

Scene 5

LIGHTS COME UP.

JEB is lying on the floor, groaning in pain, when LOUISE, DAN and CATHY all arrive at the front door. LOUISE is chatting with her brother, DAN, and his wife, CATHY, as she searches for her keys in her rather large purse.

LOUISE

I can't find my keys.

DAN

I can't imagine how you could lose them in that purse?

LOUISE

Very funny. *(Pauses while searching)* They're in here somewhere. *(Pauses while she continues to search)*

CATHY

Is Jeb home?

LOUISE

I don't think so his car's not here.

CATHY

Didn't you say something about his car breaking down?

LOUISE

Ohh yeah....that's right. His car did break down. Maybe he is home.

LOUISE KNOCKS on the door. JEB looks up but can only groan in reply. LOUISE knocks again.

LOUISE

(Shouting)

Jeb, are you home? JEBBB! Open the door I don't have my keys.

JEB

(Shouting back)

I can't move.

CATHY

I think I heard something.

LOUISE

(Shouting)

JEBBB! Open the door. It's me...Louise.

JEB

(Shouting back)

I'm trying to tell you that I can't move.

JEB begins dragging himself toward the door.

JEB

(Crawling to door)

I'm coming.

DAN

Maybe something's wrong?

LOUISE

What could possibly be wrong....other than the fact that I've married someone who is a complete idiot.

CATHY

Louise!

LOUISE

Well...he always does stuff like this. Why couldn't he just come and open the door like a normal person?

JEB finally reaches the door and reaches up to turn the doorknob, opening the door.

LOUISE

I don't know what you think you're doing sweetheart, but I've about had it with you and your crazy games.

JEB
(Weakly)
I fell on that stupid throw rug of yours and I think my back has completely gone out...in case you want to know.

CATHY
You poor thing.

LOUISE
He is such a rotten actor. I'll get you some aspirin.

LOUISE EXITS.

JEB
I had to literally crawl across the room.

DAN
Here...let me help you.

JEB
Careful....

CATHY
(To DAN)
I'll take this side and you take that side.

JEB
Easy...easy.

DAN
Don't worry we got you.

JEB
Take me to the couch. I think I can sit up.

DAN and CATHY ease JEB over to the couch.

CATHY
Are you okay?

JEB
NO! No...I am not okay. I've just lost my biggest account, and probably my job too. My Blackberry has been stolen, my daughter is spending Christmas

with her boyfriend, my car has broken down, my TV has decided not to work just in time for the biggest game of the year. And to add to all of that I've done God knows what to my back, and once my wife finds out I've lost my job, she is probably going to leave me....*(Sarcastically)* Are you okay? NO. N....O. I am NOT okay!

CATHY

My...you have had a rough time. Jeb, I know that this may seem hard for you to believe....but Jesus still loves you.

JEB

OH...He does? Does he now? Well that's just great. Cathy, you know, I think that I would have a very Merry Christmas if you would just leave Jesus out of this, thank you.

JEB angrily stands up, but then realizes that his back still hurts, and bends over in pain.

JEB

Excuse me...but I'm think I'm going to head out to find someplace to watch the game and drink in a little Christmas spirit...if that's okay with you.

CATHY and DAN step out of JEB'S way as he stalks out the DOOR.

CATHY

Sweet Jesus, I think you and I have some work to do.

DAN

You got that right.

LIGHTS FADE OUT.

<u>SONG</u>

Scene 6

LIGHTS COME UP.

THE BERNDT LIVING ROOM. DAN is sitting on the couch with a cup of coffee and reading a newspaper.

JEB ENTERS holding glass of water and a bottle of aspirin. DAN puts down the paper and watches JEB swallow a couple of aspirin and down them with a large gulp of water.

DAN

Rough game, I see.

JEB

Yeah.

DAN

Says here in the paper that they haven't lost a game by forty points in more than twenty five years.

JEB

Has it been that long?

DAN

Well look at the bright side. At least it wasn't a shutout.

JEB

Whoopie. A field goal with thirty seconds left.

DAN

So...uh...tried a bit of "grape" to ease the pain?

JEB

Yes I did. But whatever it was, it wasn't strong enough. What was needed was a nice general anaesthetic....maybe something like propofol or diazepam. Y'know something strong enough to induce a coma.

DAN

Umm.

JEB walks over to sit down in the chair.

JEB

If I have many more days like yesterday...I think I will just check myself out. Gone. No more pain.

DAN

Yeah....but then you'd really have a problem.

JEB

Huh?

DAN

Then where would you go?

JEB

What'da'ya mean where would I go? I'd be dead. I wouldn't be goin' nowhere.

DAN

I don't think so. Think you'll be going to one of two places.

JEB

Ah...you mean....

DAN

Yep. One's called Heaven and one's called Hell.

JEB

Well...y' know I just don't believe in that stuff.

DAN

Well, Jesus, certainly did. He taught the reality of Heaven...and Hell...throughout His ministry. Both before, during, and after His death on the cross.

JEB

I knew you'd find a way to bring Jesus up this Christmas.

DAN

Jeb, let me ask you just a few simple questions. Okay?

JEB

Look Dan, I don't want to argue with you.

DAN

Just humor me for a minute. Okay? And I won't ever bring Jesus up to you again. Okay?

JEB

Now THAT would be worth it. Okay. Go ahead.

DAN

Okay. Can you accept that Jesus was a real man who lived in history?

JEB

Well...I won't argue with that.

DAN

What about the twelve disciples? That from just twelve simple uneducated men, God has grown a Church with billions of believers.

JEB

Look. I don't know if there were twelve disciples or however many. All right? And....and I think it's great that Christianity exists. It's a nice religion and you've got lots of good...and y'know moral rules and all that. But you are not going to convince me that five thousand people were fed from a loaf of bread or....or that Jesus walked on water....or any of that stuff.

DAN

Why not?

JEB

Because. *(Pauses)* I just don't believe in miracles.

DAN

Well..Jeb...all God asks is that you believe in one miracle.

JEB

Yeah? Which one would that be?

DAN

Jesus' resurrection from the dead.

JEB

How could you possibly believe that?

DAN

Simple. Because it was witnessed by over five hundred people.

LIGHTS FADE OUT.

<u>SONG</u>

Scene 7

LIGHTS COME UP.

THE BERNDT KITCHEN. CATHY has on an apron and is making some Christmas cookies. She is patting and rolling out the dough on a tall kitchen island.

JEB ENTERS.

JEB

Boy, that smells really good.

CATHY ENTERS.

JEB

Now that's getting me into the Christmas spirit.

CATHY

Well, it's about time. Here have a cookie.

JEB

Thanks. *(Starts eating)* Cathy, let me ask you a question. How did you become a Christian?

CATHY

Hmm. That was a long process. But let me tell you where it all started with me: "The heavens declare the glory of God; the skies proclaim the work of His hands. Day after day they pour forth speech; night after night they display knowledge."

JEB

What does that mean?

CATHY

It's Psalm 19.

JEB

Oh. Really?

CATHY

Yeah. What it means is that God reveals Himself throughout creation. So no one has an excuse. No one. They can't claim they didn't know about God. I mean look around you, Jeb.

JEB

So you mean, even though I haven't actually "seen" God, I should know He exists.

CATHY

Yes. That's right. You don't think this entire creation was just an accident, do you? *(Pauses)* Have another cookie.

JEB

Thanks.

CATHY

You know about Monarch Butterflies?

JEB

Those are the orange and black ones?

CATHY

Yeah. Beautiful aren't they? Well Monarch Butterflies migrate every winter from locations in North America to Mexico or to Florida, and then they head back north. Just like snowbirds. But they only live about two months, you see.

JEB

Y' mean the snowbirds?

CATHY

No, silly, the butterflies. So the problem is: how do they know where to go? By the time they head north and then it's time to head back south, the first generation of butterflies have all died, and so have the second generation. So on the trip back you're into the third or fourth generation of butterflies. Well... so how do they know where to go?

JEB

Beats me.

CATHY

It's a God thing. And when you think about the vastness and complexity of creation, surely you must acknowledge that God Is and that He has created us.

JEB

Maybe.

CATHY

And you wanna know what's so amazing?

JEB

What?

CATHY

Despite the vastness of creation, and the enormity of time, Jesus told us that God knows even the number of hairs on your head.

JEB

Now if that were true....that would be amazing.

CATHY

Well it is true. You can bank on it. Jesus own words. All you have to do is trust in Him.

JEB

But that's just so hard to do. I mean how do you do that...it's not rational. How can God expect you to trust Him, when you can't even see Him?

CATHY

You can see Him all around you, His glory is everywhere. Look, how would you feel if someone didn't trust you? Not very good huh?

JEB

No, I guess not.

CATHY

Well...how do you think God feels when someone doesn't trust Him? After all He did...in the person of Jesus, leaving the glories of heaven to come live among us...so that He could show us how much He loved us. I mean, even though we keep sinning against Him and we keep disobeying His commands; and throughout time we have rejected His love. He has shown us that all we have to do is trust Him and His way of providing for us to be with Him. It's so simple it's crazy!

JEB

I wish I could. I wish I could.

CATHY

Well....why don't you just pray about it? Just in the quiet of your room, ask God to teach you how to trust Him. If you pray that, and mean it, I believe that God will answer that prayer.

JEB

You really believe that?

CATHY

That's how I became a Christian. It all started with a simple prayer like that.

JEB

Hmn.

CATHY

Try it. He won't let you down. *(Pauses)* Here, try another cookie too.

LIGHTS FADE OUT.

SONG

Scene 8

LIGHTS COME UP.

DAN is seated on the couch reading the newspaper. JEB comes in whistling and obviously in a good mood. DAN puts down the newspaper and watches JEB with increasing puzzlement and curiosity as JEB goes about his activities in high spirits.

DAN

Well you're certainly in a good mood this morning.

JEB

Am I? Oh....well, I guess I am.

DAN

Well something has happened. What's' up?

JEB

Well. I guess something has happened. Yesterday, Cathy and I had a little... talk...about some things and I thought about some of the things she said and... uh....ultimately before I went to bed I made a decision and said a little prayer asking Jesus to come into my life and to help me learn how to trust Him.

DAN

(Jumping up)

That's great. Cathy and I have prayed for that for years.

JEB

You have?

DAN

Absolutely!

JEB

I didn't know that. Well, I guess that your prayers have been answered. After I prayed, I didn't know what to expect. There were no flashes of lighting or thunder or anything, but I definitely felt a special sense of peace. And then this morning....I found this Bible collecting dust on the shelf, and I started reading it. And....here's the interesting part. It's almost like this glaze over my eyes went away, and I felt like I was understanding it for the first time.

DAN

That's a very good sign. Sounds like the Holy Spirit is helping you.

JEB

Holy Spirit?

DAN

Yes, once you believe in and accept Jesus as the Christ, He promised us that He will send you the Holy Spirit to live within you and to be your helper.

JEB

Oh? Well, great, there's a lot of things that I certainly don't understand about all of this.

DAN

The first step is believing, and then, later will come knowledge and understanding.

JEB

So...uh...now what?

DAN

What do you mean, now what?

JEB

Well...how do I make all of my problems go away. God's gonna help me do that right?

DAN

Uh, Jeb, I hate to tell you this, but just because you become a Christian doesn't mean that all of your problems are going to go away. In fact, sometimes becoming a follower of Christ can make life more difficult.

JEB

More difficult?

DAN

(Nods)

JEB

More difficult than it already is?

DAN

Maybe, only time will tell. It's all in God's hands. Listen, you ever heard of a man named Job?

JEB

Job? You mean the guy in the Bible?

DAN

Yeah, that's the one. You think you've got it bad? Well Job lost everything most of us think are important: his house, his lands, all of his possessions, his health, and even his children. His so called friends told him that he should just curse God and die.

JEB

Wow.

DAN

But he didn't do that. Despite all his troubles, Job decided that his faith in God was the most important thing in the world. And in the end God rewarded that faith. Job got back everything he lost, twice over.

JEB

Do you think that kind of faith will work for me?

DAN

Whatever happens, just put your trust in Him, He'll be with you through every trial and tragedy, and He won't let you bear more than you can handle.

JEB

Well...that's certainly good to know. I mean right now, my life's a mess. I don't know what else could go wrong. And....I really don't think I can handle anything more.

LIGHTS FADE OUT.

<u>SONG</u>

Scene 9

LIGHTS COME UP.

JEB is seated on the couch reading a book on a KINDLE. LOUISE ENTERS with some scrapbooking items. After fussing over them a few minutes she becomes curious about what JEB is doing.

LOUISE

Why aren't you watching football today?

JEB

Nothing I was interested in watching. Besides the projection bulb is out.

LOUISE

YOU....not interested in watching a football game?

JEB

No...uh...not particularly.

LOUISE

So do you like the Kindle? What are you reading?

JEB

Oh, I absolutely love it. Just what I wanted.

LOUISE

Are you sure? I can take it back and get you an Ipad?

JEB

No, no. This is great. I love it. I...uh..already downloaded this book, it's called the "Purpose Driven Life" by Rick Warren. It's excellent, very easy to read on this.

LOUISE

Wow. You really have changed, haven't you?

JEB

I guess I have.

LOUISE

(Takes a deep breath)

Listen, I guess I owe you an apology for y'know...how I reacted the other day.

JEB

Louise...you don't have to. I have done a lot of things over the years that uh.... have added up. I guess I haven't been the best husband in the world and uh....I'm going to try to change that.

LOUISE

Me too. Maybe we can try to change things together?

JEB

You haven't been a very good husband either?

LOUISE

JEB!

JEB

Sorry. Couldn't help it. *(Chuckles*) Sounds good. Give me a hug.

JEB and LOUISE hug.

LOUISE

By the way, didn't you know we have a spare projection bulb?

JEB

We do?

LOUISE

Yeah. You know me, I plan everything. I knew that they only last a couple of years so I bought a spare one a while ago. It's in that box for spare light bulbs in the utility room.

JEB

You little...you mean I could've watched the game right here at home? No. Never mind, I am a new person now

There is a KNOCK on the DOOR by a POLICEMAN.

JEB

Who could that be? I'll get it. Hold this. *(Hands Kindle to LOUISE)*

JEB walks over to the door and answers it.

JEB

Yes. Can I help you with something officer?

POLICEMAN

Well, actually I've think I've got some good news for you, Mr. Berndt. You filed a stolen property report two days ago and uh....looks like we've found your property: One Blackberry Curve? *(Hands phone to JEB)* Can you identify it for us? *(Hands phone to JEB)*

JEB

(Examines phone)

Yes! This is mine. I recognize this scratch right here....let's see. Yep, got my name and number. This is great! How did you find it?

POLICEMAN

Looks like we had a lucky break in the case. One of our officers found a juvenile with a backpack rifling through a car and after stopping him, found your phone in the backpack along with some other stolen goods. Since it is the holiday season, we thought we would try to personally deliver those items back to their rightful owners.

JEB

Well...I've very grateful officer, I don't know how to thank you.

POLICEMAN

You already have. Just sign this property receipt right here.

JEB signs the receipt.

POLICEMAN

Very well. I'm off to the next stop. Uh...happy holidays.

JEB

Merry Christmas!

POLICEMAN

Yes...of course....you're right....Merry Christmas.

As the POLICEMAN EXITS, CATHY AND EMMA ENTER and walk to the door, passing the POLICEMAN.

CATHY

Look who we brought.

JEB

What on earth? EMMA!

EMMA

Dad, after I heard what happened to you, I couldn't stay. I had to come back.

JEB and EMMA hug each other.

JEB

I can't believe this. I just don't know what to say. I get my Blackberry back, Emma's home. I mean....I'm amazed.

DAN ENTERS and rushes to the door before JEB can close it, followed by TOM.

DAN

Look who I found outside!

JEB

Tom! What are YOU doing here?

TOM

I couldn't wait to let you know the good news.

JEB

What? After losing the Hardcastle account?

TOM

We didn't lose it. That's why I'm here. I spoke to Mr. Hardcastle to explain why you couldn't call him back and just all the circumstances that happened. So.. uh..anyways... he understands and he said to just call him after Christmas and he was confident that you would be able to take care of everything.

JEB

Well...I don't know what to say. I mean I thought for sure we'd lost that account and that I'd lost my job.

TOM

Jeb, you're the best rep we have. We would never fire you over...losing an account.

JEB

Well...I didn't know that.

TOM

Nonsense. It's tough out there, but we'll get through it. And we certainly need to keep good people like you.

JEB

Gee, Tom, thank you.

TOM

Say, isn't that your blue Honda with the big ugly Gator sticker on it? The one parked on Orange Avenue?

JEB

Well...I don't know if I would describe it that way, but, yes I think you are talking about my car. I haven't had a chance to get it towed yet.

TOM

Did you run of gas or something? Cause I stopped and looked inside.... and uh...well the gas gauge reads empty.

JEB

No...I was driving and the car just died on me.

TOM

Did you consider that you might have just run of gas? Because that gas gauge definitely says empty.

JEB

Oh for crying out loud. I can't believe that I just ran out of gas.

LOUISE

(Shaking head)

Some things will never change.

CATHY

Look at the good side. Now you won't have a big car repair bill!

JEB

Yeah, I guess you're right.

DAN

Jeb, looks like things have worked out pretty good for you here.

CATHY

I think it's a God thing.

JEB

Well thanks to my family, my employer, and...my in-laws....this has been a very special Christmas.

TOM

Let's go see if we can find a gas station open somewhere and get some gas for your car.

JEB

Let's do it.

TOM

Oh...I guess I should warn you. You know where the Gator sticker on your car is? Well...there's a big huge 40-0 someone spray painted in garnet and gold all over it. Oh...and a few tomahawks too. Just thought you'd want to know.

JEB

Garnet and gold? On my car? Okay, okay. I guess if I can thank God for all the good things in my life, then I can still thank Him even when something happens that's not so good.

DAN

There you go, that's exactly what Job would have said.

TOM

Well. Let's go. Merry Christmas, everybody.

ALL

Merry Christmas.

LIGHTS FADE OUT.

MESSAGE

<u>SONG</u>

Please see the [illegible] information and application at the end of this book or [illegible] and [illegible] will be [illegible] on application to Skip Martin, 1620 [illegible] Street, [illegible] Sarasota, Florida 34236, or www.christmasplays[illegible]

It's A Wonderful Christian Life

By Skip Martin

<u>OVERTURE</u>

Scene 1

LIGHTS COME UP.

PAUL hurries through the living room while searching for an unknown object.

PAUL

Carol...Have you seen my shoes?

CAROL

(From offstage)

Did you look where you left them?

PAUL

If I knew where I left them then I wouldn't be looking for them would I?

CAROL enters, also in a hurry.

CAROL

If you'd put them where they belong then you wouldn't have this problem.

PAUL

No. The problem is I put them in one place and then you have one of your cleaning fits and put them in another place. Now I have no idea where they are.

SHANNON, the GRIFFIN'S seventeen year old daughter enters.

SHANNON

Hey, Dad, can you give me $10.00? All the guys are going skating today?

PAUL

Aren't you supposed to be in school?

SHANNON

Daa...d. This is Christmas Eve. There is no school.

PAUL

Oh. That's right. *(Gets out wallet)* Look...all I've got is a $20.00.

SHANNON

(Snatches the bill)

That's okay. I'll bring you back the change.

PAUL quickly counts what's left in his wallet, as SHANNON exits.

PAUL

Well, you better or I might not have enough left to get you a Christmas present.

LISA, the GRIFFIN'S younger daughter, walks in holding PAUL'S shoes.

LISA

Dad...I just found your shoes in the washing machine.

PAUL glares at CAROL. Then walks over and takes the shoes from LISA.

PAUL

Thank you.

CAROL

Paul. Isn't it a bit late to do Christmas shopping?

PAUL

Now, don't start with me. You know I always do all my Christmas shopping on Christmas eve. I've pre-selected everything. I know exactly what I'm going to buy.

CAROL

Well...you always wait until the last minute. Someday...there's going to be a snowstorm or something and you're not going to be able to get out. Then what are you going to do?

PAUL

A snowstorm? This is Florida.

CAROL

Well...something is gonna happen so don't push your luck.

PAUL

Lisa, I didn't realize your sister liked skating so much. And another thing. I haven't seen her get up this early since she found out about the Easter bunny.

LISA

Shannon, skating? No way. I think she's going somewhere with Billy Johnson.

PAUL and CAROL

Billy Johnson?

PAUL

That does it. That does it. My daughter is seeing way too much of that Billy Johnson.

CAROL

Lisa, honey, where is she going with Billy Johnson?

LISA

She wouldn't tell me. She said it was a secret.

PAUL

That really does it. I'm going to ground her for a week. No...for a month. No... for a year!

CAROL

Now, Paul. Calm down. We don't know what's going on. Let's wait until we talk to Shannon and get all the facts.

PAUL

You want facts? Fact one: Billy. Fact two: Johnson. There. Now you have all the facts.

CAROL

Paul...I think your overreacting...

PAUL

(Grabs coat)

Well...right now I don't have time to overreact. I've got Christmas shopping to do. Okay. We'll take about this later.

PAUL walks out the door. As CAROL walks over to LISA, PAUL opens up the door.

PAUL

Do you know where I can find a chastity belt?

LIGHTS FADE OUT.

<u>SONG</u>

Scene 2

LIGHTS COME UP.

PAUL is carrying a huge pile of packages. He struggles across stage and then roughly sets the pile down.

PAUL

(Singing)

OH...this is the most terrible time of the year.

PAUL gets out his list and starts checking things off. As he is doing this, PAUL's cellular phone starts ringing. PAUL starts looking for it and finds it in his briefcase at the bottom of the pile of presents.

PAUL

How am I supposed to finish this if you keep interrupting...Oooh, Mr. Bailey. I didn't realize it was you. The Jones account? Well that's the one we had to redo, remember? He didn't? Well..we can change that. He doesn't...Mr. Bailey... don't be too hasty... Mr. Bailey it's Christmas Eve...Mr. Bailey...Mr. Bailey.

PAUL slowly hangs up the phone and sits down.

PAUL

I don't believe it. I don't believe it. It's Christmas Eve and I've been fired. Ho, ho, ho. Merry Christmas.

As PAUL slowly starts picking up his packages, two teenage boys run by and grab a couple of his packages. They begin tossing the packages back and forth.

PAUL

Hey. Hey. What' ya doin? Those are mine.

FIRST BOY

Whoa, dude. I think he wants them.

SECOND BOY

Hey man, we found these. Finders keepers!

PAUL

Now look. Put those back.

FIRST BOY

You want them back. Okay. How much money you got?

PAUL

(Starting to reach into pocket)

I'm not going to give you any money. Now put those down.

SECOND BOY

(Menacingly)

Oh, a tough guy. Let's see how tough you are. You gonna fight us?

PAUL

I'm not going to fight you.

FIRST BOY

Oh...why not. You afraid of us?

PAUL

No. I'm not afraid of you. I just can't. It's against my faith.

SECOND BOY

Against your what?

PAUL

Against my faith.

FIRST BOY

Hey are you one of those Christian freaks?

PAUL

Yes. As a matter of fact, I am a Christian.

SECOND BOY

Okay, Mr. Christian. Let's see what you got in here.

The FIRST BOY stands menacingly between PAUL and the SECOND BOY as the SECOND BOY tears apart one of the packages. He reaches in and pulls out a...very DOWDY NIGHTGOWN.

SECOND BOY

(Giggling)

We'll looky here. That's pretty rad man.

FIRST BOY

Whoooee! Does your wife know about this?

PAUL

That's for my mother-in-law.

FIRST BOY

Gonna fight us now? Winner takes all. Come on. Come on.

The FIRST BOY taunts PAUL, poking at his face. The SECOND BOY turns around and squats with his posterior in the air.

SECOND BOY

Hey, man. Hey, man. I'll give you a free kick. All you gotta do is kick me man.

PAUL is angry enough to do it. He starts forward, but then realizes that he cannot.

PAUL

Here, you want the nightgown? Take it. If you want it that bad, take it all.

The BOYS look at each other and shrug. Then giggling to themselves they go for the pile of gifts and gather up as many as they can, then head downstage.

FIRST BOY

Sucker.

SECOND BOY

Hey, you can have the nightgown. *(Tosses at Paul)*

The BOYS exit.

PAUL kicks one of the remaining gifts and slowly slumps down.

PAUL

I don't believe it. I don't believe it. Oh...God...where are you now? Where have you been? Please help me. *(Pauses)* I wish I wasn't a Christian.

As PAUL sits there, distraught, an older woman, who is clearly a bag lady enters.

ANGEL

Oh...dear. This is worse than I thought. *(Pauses)* Ahem. *(Waits)* Ahem. Excuse me sir.

PAUL looks up to see who is talking.

ANGEL

I believe you requested some help.

PAUL

(Confused)

Help? Me? Oh...I was talking to myself.

ANGEL

(Pulls out index card)

You are Paul Griffin? Birthdate: April Seventeen...in the Year of Our Lord One Thousand Nine Hundred and Sixty One.

PAUL

Have we met before? How did you know my name?

ANGEL

Well, Paul, it's like this. I'm your guardian angel.

PAUL

(Laughing)

You're my what? You're my guardian angel? Sweet, really sweet. Look I've just been fired. I've been assaulted. Had my presents stolen and I've been subjected to a gang of carolers singing that "This is the most wonderful day of the year". Now, I'm talking to a bag lady who thinks she's an angel. Look if its money you want. You can have everything I've got. Here...two dollars. That's it. That's all I've got! Take it. Take it and drink some more of that joy juice you've been drinking.

ANGEL

Paul...remember when you where a little boy? You used to love Rudolph. Rudolph, the Red-Nosed Reindeer. You used to sing that song all the time. You liked it because you had all those allergies and the kids always used to tease you about having a red nose.

PAUL

What? Hey...lots of people liked that song, and lots of kids have red noses.

ANGEL

Paul... remember when you first became a Christian. Before that, you had always believed in looking out for Number One. But...that's only because you didn't understand what Christianity was all about. You then became curious. You wanted to know why people became Christians. So you decided to get a book; to find out what Christianity was all about. I was there at the bookstore. I helped you pick that book.

PAUL

What are you trying to pull? Lots of people know I became a Christian after reading a book.

ANGEL

Yes. But do they know the book was "Beyond Ourselves" by Catherine Marshall?

PAUL

Well...

ANGEL

Do they know the bookstore was Woodland Books in Sunnyvale, California.

PAUL

No...but..

ANGEL

How 'bout the book you almost bought, but you ended up putting back? Remember? "New Age Reason" by Shirley McLaine.

ANGEL

Why do you think you changed your mind? Why did you switch those books? Paul, I was there. I helped you change your mind.

PAUL

Listen, lady. You know how many people I've told that story to?

ANGEL

Remember when you took your Dad's favorite watch and broke it? You were so scared he'd find out that you broke it that you buried it in that dirt lot up the road. *(Pauses)* He looked all over for that watch...looked for days. But, you never told him did you? You've never told anybody about that watch have you?

PAUL

I'd forgotten about that watch. I've never...I've never told anybody.

ANGEL

(Holds up watch)

Isn't this the watch?

PAUL

What is going on here? Who are you? I must be having a nightmare. Come on Paul. Wake up. Okay. You can wake up now.

ANGEL

Paul, you're not having a dream. And you're certainly not having a nightmare. But as your guardian angel, believe me when I tell you that without Christ, your life truly would have been a nightmare. Paul...I'm here because its important for you to realize that becoming a Christian was the best thing that ever happened to you.

PAUL

Well Christianity certainly isn't doing me much good right now.

ANGEL

Entering into a life with Christ doesn't mean that bad things won't still happen to you. In fact, sometimes, being a follower of Jesus will actually cause you to suffer. Look in your Bible. Read about the lives of Paul, Peter and the Twelve. They all suffered greatly for the cause of our Lord.

PAUL

Yeah, yeah, yeah. But at least they didn't have to put up with Christmas.

ANGEL

Paul..I know you didn't mean that.

PAUL

Whatever.

ANGEL

Without the first Christmas, there would be no Christ. Without Christ, there would be no Christmases. And then there would be no wonderful Christmas memories. Come...take my hand, I'm going to take you on a journey through some of your Christmas memories.

PAUL

Look...lady. I'm really not in the mood for this. Do I have to?

ANGEL

I'm afraid you really have no other choice.

LIGHTS FADE OUT.

<u>SONG</u>

<u>SONG</u>

Scene 3

LIGHTS COME UP.

PAUL

I'd forgotten about that Christmas. That's the one where I met my wife...Carol. Now that was a good Christmas. I took her home to meet my parents. I'd only known her for three weeks. But I knew...she was gonna be the girl I was going to marry.

ANGEL

You didn't take Carol home to meet your parents Paul.

PAUL

What do you mean? It was that Christmas. Yeah, that's the one...I met her in Church...right after Thanksgiving.

ANGEL

You didn't meet her Paul. You didn't meet her because you weren't a Christian. Remember, you said you wished you never were a Christian? Well, your wish has been granted.

PAUL

Ah that's right...you're a guardian angel. You grant wishes. Well...I probably would be better off.

ANGEL

You didn't meet her Paul, because you weren't going to church. Not First Church, not any church. Carol came to First Church a couple of times, but she didn't meet you so she quit going. She ended up marrying a fellow she met at a local bar, you may have heard of him: Joe Hammond.

PAUL

Joe Hammond? Carol married Joe Hammond? I can't believe that. The guy was a con man. And a politician.

ANGEL

It wasn't a happy marriage. Joe had too much money and too many mistresses. Unfortunately, they ended up losing everything after his indictment.

PAUL

That's terrible.

ANGEL

That's not the worst of it.

PAUL

It gets worse than that?

ANGEL

Much worse. You see, Carol had such a hard life, that she never ended up meeting someone she trusted. Someone that could tell her about Christ in a way that she could understand and believe.

PAUL

So what happened to her?

ANGEL

Come see for yourself.

The ANGEL motions to PAUL to walk to the side of the stage. A light comes on to reveal CAROL as she is cleaning an establishment.

PAUL

She's a maid? Well...she was good at cleaning.

CAROL finishes her work and looks around wistfully then prepares to leave as the lights go off.

ANGEL

Come. Let's go to a place where they celebrate Christmas for twelve days.

LIGHTS FADE OUT.

<u>SONG (The Twelve Days of Christmas is the song originally performed)</u>

<u>SONG</u>

Scene 4

LIGHTS COME UP.

ANGEL

Did I mention to you that I had the privilege of being there on the night that Our Savior was born?

PAUL

You're kidding. You were actually there? Naw. You're kidding me..

ANGEL

No. I am most certainly not joking. Look I can prove it. *(Reaches into her bag and hands a paper to PAUL)*

PAUL

(Examines paper carefully)

These autographs aren't real. But I'll grant you this. That was a Christmas worth celebrating.

ANGEL

Every Christmas is worth celebrating. When Christ was born, He was God's everlasting gift to mankind. Through His life and death, came the opportunity for salvation to everyone who accepts it. And with salvation, comes victory over death and life everlasting with our Blessed Lord and Savior. A life more wonderful than we can imagine.

PAUL

Yeah, yeah. Look I know all that. But its so hard to put all your faith in that. To trust that it's really true.

ANGEL

Faith in a concept is hard. But Faith in a Person you know is not. Come. Let us go.

LIGHTS FADE OUT.

<u>SONG</u>

<u>SONG</u>

<u>SONG</u>

Scene 5

LIGHTS COME UP.

PAUL

Seeing that child reminds me of when my children were born. I'll never forget when Shannon had just arrived. She was a Christmas baby. As I was holding her...she looked up...trembling...frightened...those big brown eyes looking up at me. I just wanted to take her into my arms and protect her...forever.

ANGEL

You didn't have any children Paul.

PAUL

You mean Shannon was never born?

ANGEL

Not Shannon. Not Lisa. You see, you didn't want any children. Didn't want the responsibility. Didn't want to be tied down. Without a family, you became like a tumbleweed, always looking for a better job, looking for a better life, but never finding it. A life without Christ is a pretty empty thing.

PAUL

It's been so long that I'd forgotten how bleak life without the Lord can be.

ANGEL

Well...they don't call it Hell for nothing. Without Jesus, the most terrifying moment comes, when at the end, you look back and see that everything you've done, all that you have accomplished has been nothing...it's all been chasing the wind.

PAUL

That's so depressing.

ANGEL

But it doesn't have to be. The good news is that with the birth of that baby, Jesus, everything can change. That is the beauty of Christmas. That is why we sing Noel.

LIGHTS FADE OUT.

SONG

SONG

Scene 6

LIGHTS COME UP.

PAUL

Tell me, is it too late to change a wish?

ANGEL

Not as long as you still have some breath in your body.

PAUL

Well...then I wish that I had never said that.

ANGEL

Said what?

PAUL

You know,,,that I didn't want to be a Christian.

ANGEL

Ah..that. Well that was a very foolish thing to say. You see, Paul, when you took that very first step, on faith, to follow Christ, you became a new person, and after that history changed forever. As a Christian...you've impacted many people for the better in more ways than you can imagine.

PAUL

I never realized that I had such an effect on Carol or the kids.

ANGEL

Oh, but you did. And it was not just your family. Remember those boys that stole your Christmas presents?

PAUL

Boy, do I.

ANGEL

Well...one of them remembered you years later, and he repented, and he too came to accept Christ into his life.

PAUL

That's great. What about the other boy?

ANGEL

Sadly, not everyone can be saved.

PAUL

Can we go back now? I'd really like to be with my family and just tell them how much I love them.

ANGEL

The Good Book says, "Ask and you shall receive". I've just been waiting for you to ask. Come on, let's go. And Paul, remember, whenever things are down...don't worry, your guardian angel is looking out for you.

LIGHTS FADE OUT.

SONG

Scene 7

LIGHTS COME UP.

PAUL

Merry Christmas, everybody.

CAROL

Paul, where have you been? We've been worried about you.

PAUL

Worried about me? Carol you should never worry about me...I've got the best guardian angel in heaven.

CAROL

(Laughs)

Guardian angel? Are you all right? Well...has your guardian angel told you that Mr. Bailey has been trying to get ahold of you for the last several hours?

PAUL

Uh...Mr. Bailey...Listen Carol...I've been thinking. I can get another job. Everything will work out fine.

CAROL

You don't have to get another job Paul. Mr. Bailey called and explained the whole thing. He said he wanted to apologize for being so upset. He said he realizes that you are the best employee he has ever had and not only does he want you to come back...I think he might be giving you a raise.

PAUL

(Hugging Carol)

You're kidding.

CAROL shakes head.

PAUL

You're not kidding? That's great!

LISA

Does this mean we can open presents now?

PAUL

Well about those presents...I ran into a little problem...

SHANNON bursts in.

SHANNON

Mom...Dad...there's something I need to tell you. Something...I've wanted to tell you for a long time.

PAUL

We know.

SHANNON

You know? About the Singing Christmas Tree? How did you...

CAROL

Singing Christmas Tree? We're talking about Billy Johnson.

SHANNON

Billy Johnson? What does he have to do with...OH...*(Laughing).* Oh...Mom... no. I've got a special part in the Singing Christmas Tree. I'm singing a solo. I've been going to the rehearsals for months, but I wanted to keep it a secret so it would be a surprise.

CAROL

Is that what you've been doing all this time with Billy Johnson?

SHANNON

Yes, Mom. I couldn't tell you exactly what I was doing, because that would have ruined everything. I hope you'll forgive me if I worried you.

PAUL

So...you and Billy Johnson...no skating..no hanky panky...

DAD

DAAAD! That went out of style a long time ago. And this answer is no.

PAUL

Well... I was just concerned about you.

SHANNON

(Hugs father)

I know. And I appreciate the concern.

PAUL

Well...as I was saying about those presents...I don't have any. I mean I bought them all and...uh....I was on my way home....and...uh...I was robbed...by these two hoodlums. And then I met my guardian angel....and...

LISA

(Walks right up to PAUL with arms folded)

Dad. Do you expect us to believe that?

PAUL

But...it's true...all of it...

CAROL

Ha! I knew this would happen. I knew it.

PAUL

What?

CAROL

For eighteen years I've been waiting for this to happen because you always wait to the last minute to do your shopping.. Well now its happened. I knew it would. I've known that something sometime was going to happen and you weren't going to get your presents. So you know me. I've been prepared.

PAUL

Carol. What are you talking about?

CAROL walks over to the closet, and with much aplomb, opens the door to reveal a pile of presents.

CAROL

TA....DA. I've got backup presents from you to everyone.

PAUL

(Stunned)

You've got backup presents from me...to everyone?

CAROL nods beaming.

PAUL

You've been doing this for eighteen years?

CAROL nods still smiling.

PAUL

I don't believe it. I can't believe this. I've married a nut.

PAUL and CAROL embrace, joined by the GIRLS.

PAUL

But...I'm very happy I married a nut.

CAROL

You're very welcome.

SHANNON

Come on guys. It's time to go to the Tree. Let's go.

PAUL

All right. Let's go. Let's go everybody.

The GRIFFINS grab their coats and exit. After a few minutes, the ANGEL drifts in from downstage.

ANGEL

What a wonderful Christian life! We hope your will be too. Merry Christmas everybody.

LIGHTS FADE OUT.

MESSAGE

<u>SONG</u>

Skipping Christmas

By Skip Martin

PRELUDE

SONG

Scene 1

LIGHTS COME UP to reveal the living room of the Johnson residence. It is early morning as the Johnson's are getting ready for work and school. LINDA JOHNSON enters from stage right carrying her Daytimer.

LINDA

Frank...can you deposit my paycheck? I have to take Candy to school this morning...and I can't deposit my check and make it to work on time.

FRANK

(From offstage)

Yes, dear.

LINDA

I'll leave it here...on the table. Oh...Frank...can you take the dry cleaning too? I'll leave it by the door.

FRANK

(From offstage)

Yes, dear...

LINDA

...and don't forget...I have a PTO meeting tonight.

FRANK

(From offstage)

Yes, dear.

LINDA

Frank, are you listening to me?

FRANK JOHNSON enters from stage left. He is carrying a briefcase while trying to finish tying his tie.

FRANK

What do you mean...am I listening to you? Haven't you just heard me say "Yes, dear", "Yes, dear,""Yes, dear"?

LINDA

Well...sometimes you say "Yes, dear" when you want me to think you're listening, but you're really not listening.

FRANK

Well...what do you want me to say? *(Pretends to use hand mike)* "Roger... roger...paycheck...dry cleaning...PTO meeting. Over and out."

LINDA

(Smiling)

(Pretending to use hand mike) Ten-four.

FRANK

(With exasperation)

Women.

FRANK walks over to the table to pickup the paycheck and seeing the grocery list, picks it up.

FRANK

Going grocery shopping this afternoon?

LINDA

Yes...after I take Candy to piano lessons. If there's anything else we need, just add it to the list.

FRANK

Have you checked the phone messages?

LINDA

(Impatiently)

I haven't had a chance to.

FRANK takes the list with him and walks over by the telephone where he begins reviewing the phone's caller ID list

FRANK

Have you called Bob back about the Christmas program?

LINDA

(With exasperation)

Frank. I have...not...had...any time.

FRANK

All right. But it looks like he left another message. That's the fourth message this week.

LINDA

If you would like to take over my position on the PTO, chauffeur Candy to piano, take Candy to basketball, be Junior League secretary and organize the Church choir...then I will be happy to return Bob's phone call. Candy.... CANDY. WE ARE LEAVING...THIS...MINUTE. I'm heading to the car.

LINDA picks up her Daytimer from the table and charges toward the front door. She EXITS stage left.

CANDY

(From offstage)

Coming!

CANDY rushes onto the stage from stage right carrying her backpack in one hand and hopping to put her remaining sneaker on.

CANDY

Bye, Dad.

FRANK

Bye. Have a good day.

CANDY EXITS stage left.

FRANK sits down and picks up the grocery list again.

FRANK

Too bad you can't buy more time at the grocery store. *(Crossing off an item on the list)* No, not broccoli. I hate broccoli.

After a few moments he tosses the list on the table, picks up his coat and briefcase and exits stage left.

LIGHTS FADE OUT.

<u>SONG</u>

Scene 2

LIGHTS COME UP as Frank is seated on the couch reading the paper in the Johnson's living room. LINDA enters from stage right.

LINDA

Frank. We need to talk.

FRANK

All...lll. right. What did I do now?

LINDA

You didn't do anything.

FRANK

I didn't? Whew....you had me worried.... I thought this was going to be one of those feelings conversations. Well...what do we need to talk about?

LINDA

About the Christmas program.

FRANK

Did you talk to Bob?

LINDA

No.

FRANK

Well...don't you think you should? I mean..I think he's pretty anxious to get started on rehearsals.

LINDA

Frank. I don't think I want to do the Christmas program this year.

FRANK

Not do the Christmas program? What do you mean not do the Christmas program? We've always done the Christmas program.

LINDA

Frank, I just don't want to do it. I can't do it. I've just got too much on my plate. I think...I think I just...I just want to skip Christmas this year.

FRANK

Skip Christmas?

LINDA

Yes. Skip Christmas. I read about it in a book.

FRANK

You've got to be kidding. *(Pause)* You're serious. You're really serious about this.

LINDA

I've never been more serious about anything in my life.

FRANK

I don't know what to say. I mean...how do...how do you skip Christmas?

LINDA

It's simple Frank. It's really simple. We just don't have anything to do with Christmas. We don't do the Christmas program. We don't go to all the parties. We don't do all the shopping. We don't stay up past midnight wrapping presents. We don't bring out all the decorations. Just think about it. Think of all the time we'll have. Look at all the money we'll save.

FRANK

I'm thinking, I'm thinking.

LINDA

...and with all the money we can save, maybe we could go on that skiing trip we've always wanted to go on.

FRANK

You know how much I would love to do that. But...

LINDA

But what?

FRANK

What will we tell Bob...and all the choir members at the church? And what about...what about people at work...and the neighbors. What will we tell them? I mean... what are they going to think?

LINDA

It's really very simple Frank. We'll just tell them we're skipping Christmas.

LIGHTS FADE OUT.

<u>SONG</u>

<u>SONG</u>

Scene 3

LIGHTS COME UP.

THE CHOIR MEMBERS are assembling for the Christmas program rehearsal. BOB is talking over some rehearsal details with one of the members. KRYSTAL ENTERS in a state of considerable excitement.

KRYSTAL

Pastor...pastor! You will not believe what I have just heard. I was just talking with Mary. She told me that she was talking to Sue...and Sue said that she heard it straight from Kathy that...

BOB

Krystal....please...Krystal...calm down please. And do keep in mind that discussion we had about gossip and the dangers of a loose tongue.

KRYSTAL

But...

BOB

(Holding finger up to shush her)

No, buts.

KRYSTAL

But...this is important.

KATHY enters.

KATHY

Bob. What on earth are we going to do?

BOB

What are we going to do about what?

KRYSTAL

That's what I've been trying to tell you about. Frank and Linda...they're

KRYSTAL AND KATHY

Skipping Christmas!

BOB

What on earth are you talking about?

KATHY

Frank and Linda are skipping Christmas...

KRYSTAL

...they're going on a ski trip...

KATHY

...and they're not going to any Christmas parties, not doing any Christmas shopping and...

KRYSTAL

...no Christmas decorations...

KATHY

...and most of all...no Christmas program.

KRYSTAL

They're skipping Christmas.

BOB

(Moving slowly to a chair)

No Frank...no Linda... no Christmas program. But...they've always done the Christmas program. They are the Christmas program. How in the world can anyone skip Christmas?

LIGHTS FADE OUT.

SONG

SONG

Scene 4

LIGHTS COME UP to reveal FRANK sitting on the couch reading his paper and CANDY seated at the table working on a project.

CANDY

Dad.. All my friends think that this skipping Christmas thing is...like totally weird.

FRANK

Why don't you just tell them we've become Hare Krishnas?

CANDY

Daa.....aad.

FRANK

Look. It was your mother's idea. Not mine.

CANDY

Can't you like...talk to her or something?

FRANK

Candy, I learned a long time ago that once your mother makes up her mind about something, trying to get her to change it is like trying to move a stick in the mud.

CANDY

This is going to be the worst year of my life.

There is KNOCK on the door.

CANDY

I'll get it.

CANDY rushes off stage left to the sound of the knock. After a few moments CANDY returns with the Johnson's neighbor, DAVE.

DAVE

Hey, Frank. Long time no see.

FRANK

Oh. Hi, Dave.

CANDY

Dad.. I'm going over to Lindsey's house.

CANDY starts stage left.

CANDY

(Aside)

I need to talk to someone about my VERY weird parents.

CANDY exits stage left.

DAVE

Hey. I just came by to see how things were going. I noticed you didn't have your uh... Christmas decorations up. I didn't know if maybe you need some help or something.

FRANK

Decorations? Oh...no. We're fine. We're not putting them up this year. Linda and I have decided to uh...skip Christmas.

DAVE

Skip Christmas?

FRANK

Yeah...that's right. Skip Christmas. You know...we're not putting up decorations. No shopping. No gifts. None of that stuff. We're going skiing instead.

DAVE

Oh. *(Pauses)* Gee Frank, isn't that kinda like puttin' a roach in a punch bowl?

FRANK

Well I don't know if I would put it quite that way, Dave. Look, Linda and I talked about it and we decided that Christmas is just...way to commercialized. So instead of being like everyone else: standing in all the lines, putting up with all the hassle, and spending so much money, we'll just skip it all. With all the money we'll save, we'll be able to go on the skiing trip we've always wanted to go on.

DAVE

Well...Frank, I have to hand it to you. You've got a lot of guts. I mean what with you being the only house in the neighborhood without any decorations. You know, I couldn't do that. But hey...between you and me...I could sure handle saving all the money. Even with me and Martha both working full time, we barely make it as it is. I can't imagine what we'd do if one of us lost a job.

FRANK

Tell me about it. See. That's it. That's the point. We always spend all this money on Christmas. And what for? To keep up with the neighbors? Because its what we're expected to do? We just want to get away from all that this year. Man, I can't wait to be on the slopes of Aspen while everyone else is shredding wrapping paper all over their homes.

DAVE

I'm jealous, I'm really jealous. Wish I could join you. Hey when are you leaving?

FRANK

December twenty third. Just before all the real craziness breaks out. That way we won't have to be around for the church Christmas program.

DAVE

Wow...you're not doing that either? I mean...you always do the Christmas program.

FRANK

Dave, like I said we're totally skipping Christmas this year.

DAVE

Look Frank, Martha would kill me if I didn't ask...so what if I offered to decorate your house for you?

FRANK

Thank you, but no. We are totally...

FRANK and DAVE

...skipping Christmas this year.

DAVE

Can't say I didn't try. Anyhow, if you change your mind, let me know. See ya. and uh...good luck on the slopes.

FRANK

Thanks. And good luck at the mall.

DAVE EXITS stage left.

LIGHTS FADE OUT.

<u>SONG</u>

Scene 5

LIGHTS COME UP to reveal BOB, and FRANK sitting in the living room of the Johnson residence.

FRANK

Look, Bob. We appreciate you coming over to talk to us. But Linda and I have made up our minds. Christmas has gotten too commercialized. We just don't want to do all the shopping, put up all the decorations and all that...we've just decided to skip Christmas. And you know...that includes the Christmas program.

BOB

I understand what you're saying about Christmas becoming too commercialized.. But aren't you missing something here?

FRANK

Yeah. I'm missing all the crowds at the mall. I'm missing all the stress from rushing around. It's great!

BOB

That's not what I meant.

FRANK

All right. So what's your point?

BOB

Frank. Aren't you forgetting about Jesus. Isn't He the reason we celebrate Christmas in the first place?

FRANK

Aw...Bob. Do you have to bring Jesus into this?

BOB

Yes. I'm afraid I do. Look, Frank you've been members of First Church for what...fourteen years?

FRANK

Fifteen.

BOB

All right, fifteen years. After all that time....who is Jesus to you anyways? Is He just some little baby born in Bethlehem some two thousand years ago? Or is He something more than that?

FRANK

C'mon...Bob you know me. I'm a Christian. I believe in Jesus.

BOB

Yes. I believe you understand that...up here *(points to head).* But do you really believe it in here *(points to heart)*? Because that's why we celebrate Christmas Frank. Not for all the gifts and the decorations and all that other stuff. It's because our Savior, our Living Savior, came into the world.

FRANK

Well. Yeah...but can't I celebrate Jesus on the ski slopes too?

BOB

I'm sure you can. But....

LINDA enters from stage left with a bag of groceries.

LINDA

Hi Bob. *(To Frank)* Remember what we discussed. We ARE skipping Christmas this year.

LINDA walks stage right and exits.

FRANK

(Looks at Bob and shrugs)

You heard the boss. Look Bob. If it was up to me, I would be happy to do the Christmas program this year. But...well you heard her. I'm afraid you're just going to have to find someone else to do it this year.

BOB

Look, Frank, I'm not worried about finding someone else to do the show. I'm worried about you and Linda *(Gets up to leave).* Think about it, all right. I'll be praying for you.

FRANK

Thank you Bob. I appreciate that. But be sure to pray for some good skiing weather.

BOB EXITS.

LIGHTS FADE OUT.

<u>SONG</u>

Scene 6

LIGHTS COME UP to reveal that everything is hectic at the JOHNSON household as the family finishes its preparation for their ski trip. Suitcases are piled up near the door. CANDY enters with another suitcase and puts it near her luggage stack, which is considerably larger than the other suitcase piles.

CANDY

Da...a...ad. When is Mom coming home?

FRANK enters.

FRANK

What time is it? *(Looking at watch)* She should be home by now. *(Seeing Candy's pile of luggage)* What is this?

CANDY

(Coyly)

What is what?

FRANK

(Walking over and standing behind pile)

What is...this?

CANDY

Just...stuff.

FRANK

And you think you're going to take all this...stuff? I don't think so.

CANDY

But...Da...ad, I'm gonna need it.

FRANK

This is a brief skiing trip. We'll be gone six days. You're not going on the Lewis and Clark expedition.

CANDY

I can't take all my things? This is so unfair.

CANDY walks away to sulk. LINDA enters from stage left walking very slowly. She appears somewhat dazed.

FRANK

What took you so long? You should have been home over an hour ago.

LINDA

Something happened.

FRANK

Well, what....what happened?

LINDA

I just got laid off.

FRANK

What was that? What did you say?

LINDA

I've been laid off. I lost my job.

FRANK

That's what I thought you said.

CANDY

You mean like...you have no job anymore?

LINDA

(Nods sadly)

CANDY

So like...what does that mean for us?

FRANK

It means that, first of all, that we are cancelling this ski trip.

CANDY

You're kidding right?

LINDA

I think your father is right. We don't have much choice. We're going to need to save every penny we can from now on.

CANDY

Grea.....at. Now what am I going to tell my friends?

FRANK

Tell them we researched the family tree and found out that we have a latent allergy to snow.

CANDY

Daa...d! Well....what about Christmas? Can we celebrate Christmas like we usually do?

LINDA

I don't see how we can afford to.

CANDY

(Stalking off)

I was right. This is the worst year of my life.

FRANK

(To Linda)

I think this is the worst year of all of our lives.

LINDA

Yeah. Now we're *really* skipping Christmas.

LIGHTS FADE OUT.

<u>SONG</u>

<u>SONG</u>

Scene 7

LIGHTS COME UP to reveal Main Street with several stores, each decorated in its Christmas best.

FRANK enters from stage right, ambling along slowly. He stops to take in each window display. Clearly, he is beginning to miss Christmas. He glances at his watch, indicating that he is waiting for something.

BOB enters from stage left. He is startled when he sees FRANK, but FRANK is too engrossed in his thoughts to notice BOB. BOB smiles and walks around to the side of FRANK.

BOB

Still skipping Christmas?

FRANK

(Jumps)

Geez. Bob, scared me half to death.

BOB

Sorry, I couldn't resist. Um...isn't window shopping against the rules for skipping Christmas?

FRANK

Window shopping? Oh...I guess you're right.

BOB

Besides, aren't you supposed to be out in Colorado right now? *(Makes skiing motion)* Heading down those slopes.

FRANK

Well...uh...I guess we're still skipping Christmas, but not the way we planned..

BOB

What do you mean?

FRANK

Well...Linda lost her job. And so we decided we'd better stay home and save the money. Don't know how long its gonna take for her to find another one.

BOB

That's terrible Frank. I'm truly sorry to hear that. *(Pause)* Is there anything I can do?

FRANK

Naw. We'll be fine.

BOB waits patiently, sensing that FRANK wants to tell him more.

FRANK

Listen, Bob, I've been thinking. I've really been kind of selfish. You know, wanting to skip Christmas...thinking only of myself. The way I've been acting, can I even call myself a Christian?

BOB

I guess that depends.

FRANK

That depends on what?

BOB

Well, do you believe that Jesus was God's son? That God sent Him into this world; that He was born in Bethlehem one morning more than two thousand years ago and that He lay down His very life for us?

FRANK

Yes. Yes, of course I understand all that. But...

BOB

But...what?

FRANK

I don't know that I'm really saved...that I'll have eternal life?

BOB looks at FRANK for a moment and fishes into his pants pocket for a pocket Bible. He pulls it out and hands it to FRANK.

BOB

Look at this verse. Read what is says.

FRANK

"For God so loved the world that He gave His one and only Son, that whoever believes in Him shall not perish but have eternal life."

BOB

Now you tell me. Are you going to have eternal life?

FRANK

Well yeah...I guess.

BOB

What do you mean...I guess? Read it again.

FRANK

"For God so loved the world that He gave His one and only Son, that whoever believes in Him shall not perish but have eternal life."

BOB

Now, Frank, can you tell me, are you going to have eternal life?

FRANK

Yeah.. I think so.

BOB

You think so? You better read it again.

FRANK

"For God so loved the world that He gave His one and only Son, that whoever believes in Him shall not perish but have eternal life."

BOB

Frank, who is it that's saying those words?

FRANK

Well, Jesus.

BOB

Are you concerned that Jesus was not telling the truth when He made that statement?

FRANK

No, no...not at all.

BOB

Then Frank, are you going to have eternal life?

FRANK

(Hesitantly) Well Jesus did say it. I believe it...so I must. *(More confidently)* I am.

BOB

Good. I'm glad we got that straightened out. Now..isn't it time you started acting on that assurance?

FRANK

You're right. Of course, you're right. Bob, thanks. I'm really glad we had this talk. Oh...here *(Hands pocket Bible back)*

BOB

Keep it. Consider it a Christmas gift. Merry Christmas, Frank. Hey, I've got to go. Dress rehearsal's tonight.

FRANK

Yeah, yeah, Thanks. Merry Christmas.

BOB EXITS stage left.

LIGHTS FADE OUT.

<u>SONG</u>

Scene 8

LIGHTS COME UP to reveal FRANK is sitting in an easy chair reading a Bible. LINDA is talking on the phone.

LINDA

(Holding phone)

No Sue...I really enjoy the scrapbooking group. But Frank and I have agreed to cut back for now, you know, until I can find another job.

FRANK

FRANK looks up to LINDA and after getting her attention, points his finger at his watch.

LINDA

Listen, Sue, I have to run. No...no really, don't worry about me. I'm sure I'll find something after the holidays. No..no...we're still skipping Christmas. Okay. Well...thank you. Bye.

LINDA walks over to see what FRANK is doing.

LINDA

What is that you're reading?

FRANK

This? Oh, it's a Bible.

LINDA

Really? That's unusual for you.

LINDA sits down next to FRANK on the couch.

FRANK

Yeah, well...I was on Main Street today and I ran into Bob and uh...we had a very interesting conversation. Say...you know what? He invited us to come to the Christmas program. And since everything has changed, I was thinking... why not?

LINDA

Frank I'm not sure...I mean... everyone knows we're skipping Christmas.

THE DOORBELL RINGS. LINDA gets up, but before she can take two steps, CANDY enters from stage right and rushes through the room with headphones around her neck.

CANDY

I'll get it.

CANDY EXITS stage left.

FRANK

Who on earth can that be? It's ten at night.

A CROWD of people noisily stalk into the room. Among the crowd are BOB, KATHY, and KRYSTAL. They are carrying various gift items and cooked meals. CANDY trails behind the group.

FRANK

What on earth are you guys doing here?

BOB

Frank and Linda, you may be skipping Christmas; but Christmas is not skipping you. Gang, show 'em what you brought.

KRYSTAL

(Handing dish to LINDA)

I know that you are a vegetarian Linda. So I brought you my absolute favorite veggie dish.

LINDA

Thank you. *(Looks under aluminum foil wrapping) (To Frank*) Ummmm. Broccoli and cheese casserole.

KATHY

Oh dear. Perhaps we should have coordinated. Well...that's my favorite too.

LINDA

Oh, look at this Frank, more broccoli and cheese casserole.

FRANK

(Sarcastically)

Great. I'm really looking forward to it.

BOB

My wife made this. I apologize. I don't even know what it is.

KATHY moves over to unwrap the top of the dish. LINDA and KRYSTAL all look to see what it is.

LINDA, KATHY, and KRYSTAL

Broccoli and cheese casserole

BOB

I guess we didn't check with each other. I hope you like broccoli.

FRANK

(Grimacing)

Oh...I uh...I just love it.

BOB

Uh...we also all chipped in and got you this gift certificate. *(Hands to Frank)*

FRANK

(Reading)

A two hundred dollar gift certificate from Publix. That's great. (*To Linda)* Not bad for someone who's skipping Christmas.

KRYSTAL

Oh....and Linda. I want you to take this card. It's my uncle Louies'. He said he could offer you a job. I'm not really sure what he does. Something to do with shoes and cement...or whatever...but he's a great guy.

FRANK

(Takes card and hands to LINDA)

Sounds like an interesting prospect.

LINDA

(Visibly moved)

I hardly know what to say. It is so nice of you guys to come over and to bring us....all these things. I don't know what to say...I just can't believe you did it! I mean with us going on and on about skipping Christmas and not doing the show...aren't you just so angry with us?

KATHY

Linda, we understand why you wanted to skip Christmas. But the Christmas you wanted to skip is not the real Christmas. *This* is what it means to celebrate Christmas. To love your family, friends, and neighbors, to give something of yourself.

BOB

Kathy's right. Being able to give and care...just like this...gives life meaning. Otherwise we're not really living; we're just existing.

LINDA

Guys, I'm really sorry I decided not to do the Christmas program. I wish I had never decided to skip Christmas. Will you guys ever forgive me?

BOB

Of course we will.

THE OTHERS

Sure. Yes. Absolutely.

BOB

You know, the show's tomorrow night. It's not too late for you guys to do your thing.

LINDA

Isn't Kathy doing my part?

KATHY

Not if you'll do it.

LINDA

I can't...not without any rehearsal or anything...

BOB

We understand. But we'll see you tomorrow night, right?

FRANK

(Looking at Linda)

What 'd' ya say?

LINDA

Okay. All right. That would be nice. We'll be there.

BOB

Come on guys let's let them have some family time. Let's go.

OTHERS

Bye. See ya.

FRANK and LINDA walk everyone to the door, stage left. As they wave goodbye, FRANK notices someone in the yard.

FRANK

Dave...is that you? *(To Linda)* I think that's Dave in the yard putting lights on our tree.

FRANK EXITS the stage for a few moments, and then ENTERS once again with DAVE in tow. DAVE has a box filled with colored Christmas lights in his arms.

FRANK

Dave...what on earth are you doing in our yard?

DAVE

I'm sorry, Frank, I hope you don't mind, but I couldn't help it. Your house is the only one on the block with no lights. I heard about Linda losing her job, and well...I couldn't help it. I figured I gotta do something. So I figured....you know... what would it hurt for the Johnsons to have a few lights up. Look, I can take them down if you don't like them.

FRANK

That won't be necessary. It's just been made official as of this moment; the Johnsons are no longer skipping Christmas.

DAVE

Are you serious? That's great. That's really great. Hey, well you know...I could *really* put some lights up for you know. Like my place. All along the edge, on the rooflines too, you know. What'd ya say?

FRANK

(Looking at Linda)

Why not? You have my permission. Go for it.

DAVE

All right, great. It'll look good. I promise you.

DAVE EXITS eager to get started. FRANK and LINDA stand watching offstage as DAVE begins his work. FRANK puts his arm around his wife's shoulder.

FRANK

You know. I'm beginning to wonder why we ever decided to skip Christmas.

LINDA

I was beginning to wonder that myself.

LIGHTS FADE OUT.

<u>SONG</u>

Scene 9

BOB, KATHY, KRYSTAL, FRANK, and LINDA, are all gathered just off stage, as the Christmas show is in progress. BOB and KRYSTAL have headsets on.

KATHY

Its almost time for the last scene. You guys ready to go?

FRANK and LINDA nod.

KRYSTAL

You know after all these years, I still get chills down my back every time you guys sing.

LINDA

Kathy, are you sure this is okay? I mean you and Bill worked so hard on these parts.

KATHY

Linda...you and Frank....it's your spiritual gift. All along, I was hoping you would change your mind. I was PRAYING that you'd change your mind.

FRANK

I still don't know why we thought that skipping Christmas was such a great idea.

BOB

You're here now....that's all that matters. Besides, I'm pretty sure God has had His hand on things all along.

FRANK

Well..its clear to me that this is where we belong.

BOB

All right everybody...get ready. Remember...there are some people out there that have been skipping Christmas their whole lives, and God is depending on you to share what it's really all about. *(Listening to prompter)* That's your cue. Break a leg.

FRANK and LINDA walk across stage as LIGHTS FADE OUT. They exit on the left. The OTHERS exit stage right.

LIGHTS FADE OUT.

<u>SONG</u>

Scene 10

FRANK AND LINDA enter from stage left and cross the stage as the LIGHTS COME UP again. EVERYONE CONGRATULATES THEM. With a round of "Great job" etc.

BOB

What an ovation! Tremendous job. I knew you could do it.

KRYSTAL

I still have those chills.

KATHY

Absolutely wonderful. *(Presents Linda with flowers)* These are for you.

FRANK and LINDA

Thank you. Thank you.

BOB

I've got to talk to some folks. Don't forget about the cast party.

BOB EXITS.

KRYSTAL and KATHY

Merry Christmas. See 'ya at the party.

FRANK and LINDA

All right. See 'ya there.

KRYSTAL and KATHY EXIT.

LINDA

That was great. It never meant so much to me before.

FRANK

Yeah. Me too. But...

LINDA

But....what?

FRANK

I've been thinking. You know how we always spend so much on candy and goodies on Valentine's Day?

LINDA

Ye....s....s..s.

FRANK

...and Valentine's Day comes right after your birthday anyways.

LINDA

...and your point is...

FRANK

...well..maybe we could skip Valentine's Day this year....

LINDA

...Frank...don't even think about it.

FRANK

Yeah...I guess you're right.

KRYSTAL REENTERS STAGE

KRYSTAL

Come on guys...you don't want to *skip* the cast party.

FRANK

Very funny.

LINDA

I can see that this is never going to end.

ALL EXIT and LIGHTS FADE OUT.

DAVE'S VOICE is heard from offstage.

DAVE

Frank...Frank...FRANK.

LIGHTS COME ON to reveal DAVE staggering onto the stage. His clothes are burnt and ragged, he is covered with soot and wisps of smoke rise from his head and shoulders.

DAVE

Frank...uh...your house. There's something I have to tell you about your house!

LIGHTS FADE OUT

MESSAGE

<u>SONG</u>

Please see the royalty information and application at the end of this book. The royalty amount and availability will be quoted on application to Skip Martin, 1620 Main Street, Suite One, Sarasota, Florida 34236, or www.christmasplays.org.

Two Christmases

By Skip Martin

PRELUDE

SONG

Scene 1

LIGHTS COME UP.

JOHN RUSHMORE enters the living room in a hurry. He is carrying a piece of luggage in each hand along with a pillow under his arm.

JOHN

I'm ready.

JOHN spots a book and his reading glasses on table and struggles over to get them. He hurriedly opens his luggage to put them inside.

JOHN

Mary. Did you hear me?...I'M READ...D...DY

MARY enters also loaded down with luggage.

MARY

I can hear you. You don't have to shout so loud.

JOHN

Well it's nine twenty and were gonna be late.

MARY

Got the laptop?

JOHN
(Impatiently)

Yes.

MARY

Got your ditty bag?

JOHN
(More impatiently)

Yes.

MARY

Have the tickets?

JOHN
(Annoyed)

Yes, I have the tickets. Let's go.

MARY

Okay, all right. I'm gonna do one last check.

JOHN

C'mon. We gotta go. Our flight leaves in an hour and a half and it's the last flight to Jamaica.

MARY
(Walking around looking)

Okay...okay.

After MARY finishes checking a few things.

MARY

All right. Let's go.

JOHN

YES...all right! *(Humming)* CHRISTMAS IN JAMAICA. CHRISTMAS IN JAMAICA.

JOHN and MARY EXIT.

LIGHTS FADE OUT.

<u>SONG</u>

Scene 2

LIGHTS COME UP to reveal the Rushmore living room.

JOHN ENTERS carrying his luggage and walking very slowly. MARY ENTERS following JOHN.

JOHN

I still can't believe our flight got cancelled.

MARY

It's Christmas Eve, John, and this is Chicago. Sometimes it snows.

JOHN

I know that it snows. But we've never had a flight cancelled because of it. I just can't believe it.

MARY

Well you better get over it because it looks like we're going to have to spend Christmas at home.

JOHN

Do you realize that we've never done that before?

MARY

What?

JOHN

Spent Christmas at home. In our entire marriage we've never spent a single Christmas at home before

MARY

(With resignation)

Yes...I know.

JOHN

Maybe we can try calling the airline tomorrow?

MARY

You heard what they said. They don't expect any flights out for two days.

JOHN

I can't believe this is happening.

THE PHONE RINGS and MARY walks over to answer it.

MARY

Hello? Oh...hi, Michelle.

JOHN

(Mouthing the words)

My mother?

MARY NODS AT JOHN.

MARY

Yes....the news is right. All flights have been cancelled. *(Pauses)* No...it doesn't look like we're going to be going anywhere for a few days. *(Pauses)* Oh? Spend Christmas with you?

JOHN begins waving his hands and shaking his head no.

No...no...you are absolutely right. We never have spent Christmas with you since John and I have been married. *(Pauses)* No...no...of course not. We've always wanted to, it's just that John and I have always wanted to get away from work....and everything. *(Pauses)* No...no...actually we'd love to come.

JOHN waves his hands and shakes his head even more frantically.

MARY

What time? Sure ten o'clock sounds fine. Okay, okay. Bye. See you tomorrow.

JOHN

Mary...what did you just do?

MARY

John...John....don't get upset. Your mother had a very good point. We never have spent Christmas with your family before. Don't you think its time? After all we have been married five years.

JOHN

Yes, and there's a reason we've never spent Christmas with my family in those five years. Frankly, if it was up to me, it would be five more. I can't believe you just did that. You have no idea what you've just gotten us into. I mean Christmas with my family....is like....is like...the...ANTI-Christmas.

MARY

Come on John. It can't be that bad.

JOHN

Mary....Mary. Just trust me on this. It is.

THE PHONE RINGS AGAIN.

JOHN

Let me get it. I'll take care of this.

JOHN hastens over to the phone.

JOHN

Listen, Mom...um..look, when Mary just talked to you she didn't realize...Oh... Oh....I'm sorry...excuse me. JEAN! I thought you were my mother calling back. Uh....hello.

MARY

(Mouthing the words)

My mother?

JOHN NODS.

JOHN

Yes, that's right. The news certainly flies fast these days. *(Pauses)* No...no flights out for at least two days. Do we have any plans? Uh...no....no...not that I can think of.

MARY begins waving her hands and shaking her head no.

JOHN

Yes....I am aware of that. And actually I've felt quite badly about it. It's just that Mary and I have always felt it was important to get away from work and.... everything. *(Pauses)* Oh, of course, we would love to.. We'd love to come over.

MARY waves her hand and shakes her head even more frantically.

JOHN

What time? Oh...how about 4:00? Good. Great! We'll see you there. Okay. Bye. Looking forward to it. See ya tomorrow.

MARY

John...did you do what I think you just did?

JOHN

(Somewhat smugly)

Well...we've never spent Christmas with your family either.

MARY

Yes...and there's a very good reason for that too

JOHN

How bad can it be?

MARY

(Putting head in hands)

Bad, bad. Very BAD. John, I think I'm going to kill you.

JOHN

No you're not.

MARY

Why not?

JOHN

Because I'm going to kill you first.

MARY begins to run and JOHN chases her as LIGHTS FADE OUT.

<u>SONG</u>

Scene 3

LIGHTS COME UP to reveal the living room in the home of JOHN'S parents. This room is the picture perfect portrayal of a very commercial and worldly Christmas - the extreme version.. Christmas presents are piled high under what must be the world's largest Christmas tree and there is a second Christmas tree, aluminum with a color wheel, with even more presents piled under it.

JOHN and MARY ENTER and hand their overcoats to the MAID.

JOHN

Look...just do your best to roll with it and we'll get out of here as soon as we can.

MARY

Okay, but I don't see what could be so bad.

JOHN

You will. Trust me.

JOHN and MARY walk around to the living room, where they find DONALD, MICHELLE, BABS, RICKIE, VERONICA, CHELSEA, and GRANDMA.

MICHELLE

They're here! They're here! Merry Christmas!

There is an exchange of hugs and greetings among the family.

MARY

Hello, Michelle, Donald. It's so good to see you.

JOHN

(Eying the very large Christmas tree)

Dad...nice tree!

DONALD

Glad you like it. Each year I keep thinking...you know...we've got to get a really good tree this year. Had this baby shipped down directly from Oregon. Not bad if I do say so, huh? We've just about hit Christmas perfection! Don't you think?

MARY

I've never really seen anything quite like it...except well....y'know...maybe Rockefeller Center. It's very...uh...festive. And your outdoor light display is... is...quite impressive!

DONALD

Yeah. Started November first just to get it all done on time. Fifteen thouand lights this year. Rented a cherry picker to do the trees. *(Chuckles)* Nobody out-christmases the Rushmores!

JOHN

Yes, once Dad's on a mission, there's no stopping him.

MICHELLE

The airport called us last week to ask us to tone it down. Can you imagine? Whatever happened to the Christmas spirit?

DONALD

That's right. Santa's gotta have his runway! He's got presents to bring!

MICHELE

(Pointing to the large pile of presents)

I think there may be a present or two for you two over there.

BAB'S CHILDREN start arguing over some of the presents.

RICKIE

That's mine.

VERONICA

No it's not. It's got my name on it.

RICKIE

It says Rickie, dufus.

VERONICA

You can't even read. It says Ronnie, stupid.

CHELSEA

(Starting to cry)

What about me?

RICKIE and VERONICA

SHUTUP!

BABS

Rickie! Ronnie! Can't we share?

RICKIE

It's mine! It's mine!

Opening the present. RICKIE realizes it's a sweater.

RICKIE

(Spiking it to the ground)

A sweater? I don't want a stupid sweater.

RICKIE stomps off stage.

BABS

Rickie, darling!

DONALD

Babs, let him be. Kids will be kids.

MICHELLE

Speaking of kids. We hope you two will be making us grandparents again someday soon?

JOHN

Mom...Dad. Put a cork in it.

DONALD

Son...relax...just want to add to the Christmas shopping list...that's all.

JOHN

(Putting his arm around MARY)

We'll have one when we're ready.

BABS

Grandma...where did Grandpa go.

GRANDMA

(Dismissively)

Oh, he's off watching a football game....just like he always does.

DONALD

Well, you know Grandpa.

EVERYONE starts nodding.

GRANDPA

(From offstage)

Touchdown! Touchdown!

GRANDPA rushes ON STAGE with his arms held up.

DONALD

Wait. I think I hear him.

GRANDPA

(Running in circles)

Whoo hoo!! TOUCHDOWN COWBOYS! Whoo Hoo!

GRANDPA rushes OFF STAGE just as quickly as he entered, still cheering about a touchdown scored in the football games he is watching.

MICHELLE

All right...okay...we've had our Grandpa sighting. Now is everybody ready for lunch?

MARY

So soon? We don't go to church on Christmas morning?

DONALD

Mary, we used to go religiously. Yes sir...every Christmas and Easter. But then I started to think about it...

MICHELLE

...it's always so hard on the kids...with all their new presents and everything...

DONALD

Yes...and since we're not going to church very much the other fifty weeks of the year, Y'know? Ya gotta be consistent.

MICHELLE

Besides we've got the best Rushmore Christmas you'll ever see.

JOHN

Uh...Mom. Remember we're having dinner at the Power's, so we don't want to overdo it.

MICHELLE

Well...y'know whatever...just come on in and enjoy the spread. After all, isn't that what Christmas is all about?

DONALD

C'mon kids.

MARY

(Looking at JOHN)

Sounds delicious. I'm sure it'll be just great.

LIGHTS FADE OUT.

<u>SONG</u>

<u>SONG</u>

Scene 4

LIGHTS COME UP.

The living room of the home of John's parents. JOHN and MARY are getting ready to leave.

JOHN

So, how are you holding up?

MARY

Okay, I guess...it's just that...I'll be glad to sit down for just a few seconds and catch my breath.

JOHN

Well, that's Christmas with my parents. One big long holiday party...whether you like it or not.

MARY

I guess that's okay, but something does seem to be missing.

JOHN

Yeah. *(Pauses)* Well I'm ready to get out of here. Imagine if we got snowed in and had to stay.

MARY

We did get snowed in remember?

JOHN

Oh, yeah. That's right. Hey, let's go say goodbye.

MARY

Listen...it wasn't that bad. Your parents are sweet. Okay...maybe they have gone overboard a little bit.

JOHN

You think? Anyway, now I need a break from Christmas.

MARY

Well, you're not going to get it at my house. My parents are intense in their own way.

DONALD and MICHELLE enter.

DONALD

Well that was a real kicker of Christmas. Wish you didn't have to go so soon.

JOHN

It's only fair Dad. We felt like we had to spend time with both families.

MICHELLE

Oh, sure honey, we understand. Just wish ya had time for some egg nog.

DONALD

Yeah, Michelle makes it with a pretty good kick!

JOHN

Mom, I'm lactose intolerant. I can't drink egg nog.

MICHELLE

Right. *(Pauses)* I always forget. Well, I packed some fruitcake for ya. Can't let you go away empty handed.

MARY

Michelle, you hardly sent us away empty-handed. We could hardly get the trunk lid closed for all the presents in there.

DONALD

Well that's what Christmas is all about!

JOHN

Well...thanks. Thanks for having us over, and on such short notice.

DONALD

Aren't you glad you stayed?

MARY

It's certainly been the most interesting Christmas I can remember. Thank you for everything.

DONALD and MICHELLE

Goodbye.

LIGHTS FADE OUT.

<u>SONG</u>

Scene 5

LIGHTS COME UP to reveal the living room of Mary's parents.

JOHN, MARY, and JEAN and RICHARD POWERS all enter. JOHN and MARY are still heavily bundled up with their winter coats.

JEAN

John, it's so wonderful to see you two here on Christmas Day.

JOHN

(Brushing off snow)

Well we're glad to be here Jean. It's not quite the same as Jamaica, but it's very nice. Uh...*(motioning to gifts)* where should I put these?

JEAN

Oh...you didn't have to do that. The best gift for us is just to have the both of you here. But...uh...why don't we put them over here.

JEAN accepts the gifts and puts them next to the couch.

JEAN

Please...please sit down. Can I get you any coffee?

JOHN

No thank you. I have one cup a day and then that's it.

JEAN

Really. Just one cup?

MARY

More than one cup and he's bouncing all over the walls.

JOHN

Yeah...it's not a good thing. *(Looking around John spots a rather small Christmas tree with just a few modest fruits and nuts as decorations)* So..uh.. nice tree. It's um..very. simple.

RICHARD

Yes...thank you...you know there's sort of a story behind that. See the original custom of the Christmas tree first began in Germany. It all started with just the simple decoration of fir trees with such treats as apples and nuts for the children and then it sort of grew from there. Well over the last several years, Jean and I have tried to take Christmas back to the basics. So this tree, like the original ones, is one of the ways that we do that. Plain and simple.

MARY

Yeah...too plain and simple. You practically don't celebrate Christmas.

JOHN

Well...Mary..simple...basic. That can be a good thing.

MARY

John, look around you. Other than that *Charley Brown* tree there isn't a single decoration around here is there?

JOHN

(Looking around)

Well...no...but...

JEAN

I'm afraid that Mary is sometimes embarrassed about our simple ways.

MARY

Mom...our Jewish neighbors have more Christmas decorations than you do.

JOHN

Mary!

RICHARD

I'm afraid she's right. Some might consider us old-fashioned but we feel like we've discovered a way to celebrate Christmas in the right spirit.

JEAN

Mary, I did make some of your favorite Christmas Tree cookies just like I used to. Would you like some?

RICHARD

Now you're talking, let's go get some of Jean's Christmas Tree cookies.

MARY goes to her mother and provides her with a shoulder hug.

MARY

Sure, Mom. Let's go try those cookies.

ALL EXIT.

LIGHTS FADE OUT.

<u>SONG</u>

Scene 6

LIGHTS COME UP to reveal RICHARD, JEAN, JOHN and MARY seated in the Powers' living room.

JOHN

You know Richard. I really have to ask you about that jar in the kitchen.

RICHARD

Jar?

JEAN

He means the Christmas Jar, dear.

RICHARD

Oh...the Christmas jar. Well...son...that's a family secret. We've never told anyone about the Christmas Jar.

MARY

Dad...that's an awful lot of change. You don't need any help or anything do you?

RICHARD

No...no. It's nothing like that. It's just something that we've just kept personal that's all.

JEAN

Maybe if we tell them, Richard, they could help us with our problem.

RICHARD

You think so?

JEAN

Yes, I think perhaps they might be able to help.

RICHARD

All righty. Well I guess then...I'll tell 'em. Let's see...where should I begin? Well it all began when we retired a few years back. We were cutting back on things and decided that we wouldn't spend any more for Christmas than we could save up during the year. So Jean got this jar and whenever we had any loose change or bills we would just throw it into the jar.

JEAN

It started off slow...but then it got to be like a game and before you know it we had a little competition going to see who could put in the most change.

RICHARD

Well, Christmas time came around and we got out the jar and counted out the money and it came to exactly one hundred and thirty one dollars and twenty four cents. Not bad.

JEAN

So we decided that we would take it to the mall and that's all we were going to spend on our Christmas gifts that year.

RICHARD

Say...who's telling this story? Me or you?

JEAN

You are of course, dear.

RICHARD.

Well...thank you kindly. So we drove to the mall and I dropped Jean off near the entrance and went to park the car.

JEAN

I had the jar.

RICHARD

Yes. Jean had the jar. After I finished parking the car I walked up to the entrance where Jean was and then saw Jean and then I saw a little old lady walking away carrying our jar.

JEAN

Boy was he surprised.

RICHARD

You've got that right. I said "Jean, is that our Christmas Jar that woman is walking off with?"

JEAN

I said, "Yes it is".

RICHARD

I said "Well Jean...you've got some 'splainen to do"

JEAN

Well I just told him that I saw the poor little old lady with hardly a thing in the world just sitting there. And here we were with this jar of money about to spend it on things that we really didn't need....so I just went over to her and handed her the jar and said, "Merry Christmas". At first she didn't understand that I was trying to give her the jar, but after I insisted that she should have it, she broke into the biggest smile that you have ever seen. And then she thanked me profusely, over and over and over.

RICHARD

After I heard that story...what could I do? There was nothing to do but go home and celebrate Christmas...

JEAN

...without any presents.

RICHARD

Nope, not a single present. But that was the best Christmas we ever had.

MARY

Mom, I'm so amazed...I don't know what to say.

JOHN

That's an amazing story. But um...what about the jar in the kitchen?

RICHARD

I'm getting to that. Well...the next year we decided we would start a new Christmas Jar and save up all the change again. That year we did even better.... we saved up over two hundred dollars. But this time instead of going to the mall, we decided to keep an eye out for someone who might need our Christmas Jar for Christmas. We found a neighbor whose car needed a new battery for Christmas.

JEAN

She kept having problems with her car and was in danger of losing her job so we decided to give her the Christmas jar.

MARY

How many years have you been doing this?

RICHARD

Oh, I don't know...about six years now?

MARY

Mom, I can't believe you guys. I mean you've always been weird....but I just can't believe you've been doing this Christmas Jar thing for all this time.

JEAN

Mary, the Christmas Jar has been one of the greatest blessings we've ever experienced.. Christmas is about a very special joy. And we've been able to bring a little bit of joy to a few people at a time when they have least expected. it.

JOHN

So have you decided what you're going to do with this year's Christmas Jar?

RICHARD

That's our problem. We've haven't found the right person just yet. We were kinda hoping that you could help.

JOHN

Yeah...yeah, I think I can help. I know just the right person for that jar.

MARY

You do?

JOHN

(Getting to his feet)

Yes, I do, but if we're going to get it to 'em, we're going to have to leave like now - before it's too late.

RICHARD

All righty...then let's get going.

JEAN

Oh...this is going to be fun.

MARY

(To John)

Have you gone out of your mind?

JOHN

As a matter of fact Mary, this is the most sane thing I've done this entire Christmas holiday.

ALL EXIT.

LIGHTS FADE OUT.

<u>SONG</u>

Scene 7

LIGHTS COME ON.

RICHARD, JEAN, JOHN and MARY are walking along Main Street.

MARY

Did you see the look on that guy's face?

JEAN

He lit up so brightly I thought he was going to burst.

RICHARD

John boy...you were right. That's exactly who that Christmas Jar needed to go to this year. You could get good at his y'know?

JOHN

Nah..I don't think that's me.

RICHARD

Say...you want to look at some of the Christmas decorations on Main Street?

MARY

What..Dad! YOU resting your eyes on such pagan festivities?

RICHARD

I never said I didn't appreciate all the pretty lights and decorations. My complaint is only with the utterly greedy, commercial and artificial attitude behind it all.

JEAN

Why don't you boys take in the sights, while Mary and I head back to the house and make some good old-fashioned egg nog. *(To Mary)* Is that all right?

MARY

Is that all right with you John?

JOHN

Sure. You guys go ahead.

JEAN

Okay guys. Don't take too long.

RICHARD

We won't.

JOHN

I have to tell you Richard. This has been the most unusual Christmas Day that I have ever experienced.

RICHARD

You mean more unusual than Christmas in Jamaica?

JOHN

Definitely more unusual than Christmas in Jamaica.

RICHARD

John, there's something I have to ask you.

JOHN

O...kay.

RICHARD

You do know what Christmas is all about don't you?

JOHN

I'm not...I'm not sure what you mean?

RICHARD

I mean do you understand what Christmas is all about? Look, John. Christmas is really quite simple...it's all about just one thing.

JOHN

Oh. You mean. Jesus?

RICHARD

Yes. What do you think about Jesus?

JOHN

Well you know...I'm cool with him. He's all right y'know.

RICHARD

Listen, hear me out. He is more than just all right. We are talking about a gift from the Creator of the universe that you and I and Mary...that all of us received over two thousand years ago when a child was born in a tiny village in Israel. That child, Jesus, was God's way of reconciling man with Himself. You see in Jesus, God Himself became a man. Think about that for a second. God becoming a man.

JOHN

That is pretty hard to comprehend.

RICHARD

Yes, it is. And what's even more amazing is that He lived among us, talked with us, taught us, performed many miracles among us, which shouldn't be that surprising, because after all, although Jesus was a man, He was also fully God.

JOHN

Yeah...I've heard that stuff before, but there are some things that I never did understand. Like, why did He have to die the way He did?

RICHARD

God is love, son. God IS LOVE.. But He is also Holy and Perfect. And we have all proven over and over again that we cannot be in His presence because we are so selfish and arrogant and deceitful. *(Pauses)* So God's answer to this problem of sin in Jesus. You see Jesus chose to suffer a terrible death in order to accept for Himself our punishment for our sin.

JOHN

You make it sound so simple.

RICHARD

God has made it simple, John. All you gotta do is believe. That's all you have to do. The rest is up to God.

JOHN

We better catch up to the girls.

RICHARD

Sure...son. But listen...think about what I said...Okay?

JOHN

Sure..sure. I'll think about it.

LIGHTS FADE OUT.

<u>SONG</u>

Scene 8

LIGHTS COME UP.

The Rushmore's living room.

JOHN and MARY ENTER their own home wearing winter coats.

MARY

So this is what we've been missing every year by going to Jamaica.

JOHN

(Contemplating)

Yeah. *(Pauses)* I'm sorry about my family. That was pretty embarrassing.

MARY

Yeah, well I'm sorry about my parents...you know...being so old fashioned.

JOHN

No, no, no...that was nice. I mean that whole thing with the Christmas Jar was really really special. It uh...it uh..got me thinking.

MARY

Really, about what?

JOHN

Well...you know about this whole Jesus thing.

MARY

John, you're not getting religious on me are you?

JOHN

I don't know if I'm getting religious but your Dad...you know...some of the stuff he said makes a lot of sense to me. I'm starting to see that there might be a purpose...you know...to all this.

MARY

Yeah...I know. That Christmas Jar thing got to me too.

JOHN

Mary...tell me the truth. Didn't you feel so much better about Christmas at your parent's house...you know..without all the craziness..too many presents... and just, you know, the wrong attitude about the whole thing?

MARY

As much as I hate to admit it...yes.

JOHN

You know if we could celebrate Christmas that way...the right way...we wouldn't even need to get away to Jamaica to try to escape.

MARY

NOW you're scaring me. You're talking about giving up Jamaica?

JOHN

No...no...what I'm talking about is gaining something that's even better than some exotic island vacation. I'm talking about gaining a real purpose in life.

MARY

Well...I'm not ready for that. You...you can stay here and you can explore your navel or whatever and...just maybe I'll just have to go to Jamaica by myself. *(Mary turns and stalks off).*

JOHN

MARY!

MARY EXITS.

JOHN

This might be a little harder than I thought.

LIGHTS FADE OUT.

<u>SONG</u>

Scene 9

LIGHTS COME UP.

JOHN is seated in the living room of JOHN and MARY's HOME reading a Bible. After a few minutes MARY enters carrying something in a brown paper bag. Seeing JOHN reading, she hesitates for a few minutes and then decides to sit down to join him.

MARY

Hey.

JOHN

Oh...hey.

MARY

What'cha 'doin?

JOHN

(Holds up Bible)

Reading.

MARY

Is that a Bible?

JOHN

Yes...as a matter of fact it is.

MARY

OOO...oh. *(Pauses)* You really have changed...haven't you?

JOHN

(Nods head)

I...I feel like an entirely new person. I feel...at peace.

MARY

Wow.

JOHN

Amazing, huh?

MARY

Yeah...yeah it is. *(Pauses)* Listen, I'm sorry about how I've been behaving. I don't...I don't know how to explain it. *(Pauses)* I guess when I was growing up I was embarrassed about my parents and y'know how they seemed to be so different from everybody elses'...so I've kinda been running away from that my whole life.

JOHN

I understand.

MARY

So anyway when you changed so suddenly like that on me...I guess I kinda freaked.

JOHN

I understand.

MARY

Well you don't have to be so understanding. C'mon why don't you hit me or something? I deserve it.

JOHN

Mary, you know I won't do that. Come here, give me a hug. *(They hug for a moment)* There....that better?

MARY

Yeah...thank you.

JOHN

So what's in the bag?

MARY

Well...I've been thinking. Maybe we should start doing something different for Christmas...instead of...running away to Jamaica.

JOHN

No Jamaica?

MARY

Nope, no Jamaica...because...*(Reaches into bag to pull out a large glass jar)* TA DA...we could be doing our very own Christmas Jar!

JOHN

You're kidding?

MARY

Nope.

JOHN

You know....if we don't go to Jamaica....we could put a lot of change in that jar.

MARY

(Nodding)

Let's do it.

JOHN

Yeah...let's do it.

JOHN and MARY hug.

JOHN

THIS....is what Christmas is all about.

MARY

You know what? I think I'm going to start putting some change in the jar right now.

JOHN

Um...Mary. Before you do that, there's something I have to tell you.

MARY

What?

JOHN walks behind couch and picks up a Christmas Jar which is already partially filled with change.

JOHN

I've already started one.

MARY

John, I think I'm going to kill you!

JOHN

No, you're not.

MARY

Why not?

JOHN

Because I'm going to kiss you first.

MARY

No you're not.

JOHN

Why not?

MARY

Because you've got to catch me first.

JOHN

Are you ready?

JOHN grabs the jar starts to run off stage with the jar. JOHN EXITS.

MARY

(Yelling)

John..nnn. JOHN..NNN!

MARY EXITS running.

LIGHTS FADE OUT.

<u>SONG</u>

The Joy of Giving

By Skip Martin

<u>SONG</u>

Scene 1

LIGHTS COME UP.

MARGIE ENTERS.

MARGIE

Everybody ready? It's time to go.

LARRY ENTERS.

LARRY

Where's Josh and Katie?

MARGIE

Upstairs. JO.O.SH! KA.ATIE! It's time to go.

LARRY

We better get going. Whose car we taking?

MARGIE

Mine's a mess.

LARRY

Guess that means mine. I'll get the car started.

LARRY EXITS.

MARGIE

Come on kids. We gotta go. We don't wanta leave Grandpa waiting at the airport.

KATIE ENTERS.

KATIE

I'm ready.

MARGIE

Okay. Where's Josh?

KATIE

(Smirking)

He's working on his Christmas wish list.

MARGIE

What? It's already five pages long.

KATIE

I know.

MARGIE

Joshua Lawrence Chamberlain! You come down the stairs this minute young man.

JOSH

Okay, okay. I'm coming. I'm was loading my itunes.

MARGIE

Well I'm gonna itune you if we're late picking up Grandpa at the airport. Let's go.

MARGIE walks briskly to the EXIT.

JOSH

What does that mean?

KATIE

I dunno.

KATIE and JOSH EXIT.

LIGHTS FADE OUT.

<u>SONG</u>

Scene 2

LIGHTS COME UP.

GRANDPA ENTERS holding a large cup of coffee.

GRANDPA

Ah.h.h. Nothing like a good cup of coffee and the sports page.

MARGIE ENTERS. She is dressed and ready for work.

MARGIE

There you are Dad. You have everything you need? I've left my cell phone number by the phone in case you need to call me for any reason.

GRANDPA

Margie, I think I can manage to get by.

MARGIE

Well...I'm not worried about you. I'm worried about the kids.

GRANDPA

Well you go on to work and don't worry about a thing. I do happen to have a little experience with children you know.

MARGIE

(Kisses him on the head)

Yes, you do. All right. I've gotta go. Let me know if you need anything.

GRANDPA nods and smiles, waving goodbye. Then he heads back over to sit down on the couch and begins reading the sports page

JOSH ENTERS.

JOSH

Mornin' Grandpa.

GRANDPA

(Puts down paper)

Well there you are. Good mornin' Josh. Ready to have some breakfast?

JOSH

No thank you Grandpa, I'm just having a Cliff Bar.

GRANDPA

Cliff Bar? What's that?

JOSH

You know. It's uh...its like one of those health food bars.

GRANDPA

Health food bar. Doesn't sound very healthy to me?

JOSH

(Shrugs shoulders)

They're all right.

GRANDPA

Say....uh Josh. How come there aren't any Christmas decorations up yet?

JOSH

I dunno. Just haven't gotten around to it yet. We've been kinda busy.

GRANDPA

Yeah...well...uh...Christmas is just two days away.

JOSH

Mom, said you would help us when you got here....since you didn't have anything else to do.

GRANDPA

(Deadpans)

Oh...she said that, did she?

JOSH

Yep.

GRANDPA

Well...uh...what have you done to get into the Christmas spirit?

JOSH

I've made my Christmas wish list. Wanna see it?

GRANDPA

Well sure...absolutely.

JOSH

Okay. Be back in a sec.

JOSH RUSHES OUT and returns quickly with his wish list.

JOSH

(Unravels a large list which drops all the way to the floor)

Here it is.

GRANDPA

Wow. That's quite a list you have there.

JOSH

Wanna know what's on it?

GRANDPA

Well...

JOSH

....Okay! First I want an I-Pad. Then I want a Nerf Vortex Blaster...those are really neat. And then I want a Nintendo 3DS handheld...

GRANDPA

Hold on, hold on young man. Aren't you forgetting a little something?

JOSH

I am? What did I forget? I can still put it on.

GRANDPA

I wasn't talking about the list. I'm sure that it has everything you could possible want on it.

KATIE ENTERS.

KATIE

Oh, it does all right, Grandpa. Trust me I read it.

JOSH

(Angrily)

You read my list? I didn't say you could read it. And stay out of my room.

KATIE

Well how is anyone gonna know what to get you if they can't read your list smarty pants?

JOSH

Well you're not gonna get me anything on this list anyways.

KATIE

Well I'm not now!

GRANDPA

All right, all right. I think that's enough of that. How 'bout we make sure of Grandma's special Christmas tree cookies....just like Grandma used to make?

JOSH and KATIE

Yeah...All right.

GRANDPA

All right! Let's head to the kitchen.

ALL THREE begin to walk to the kitchen.

JOSH

Grandpa? I miss Grandma.

GRANDPA

I know son. I know. I do too.

LIGHTS FADE OUT.

<u>SONG</u>

Scene 3

GRANDPA and the KIDS ENTER the LIVING ROOM eating Christmas Tree cookies.

GRANDPA

Do you kids know the real story of Christmas?

JOSH

Which one? Rudolph the Red-Nosed Reindeer?

GRANDPA

(Shakes head)

JOSH

The Grinch?

KATIE

No. Not those stories, silly. He means like... with Joseph and Mary. Right, Grandpa.

GRANDPA

Right-o.

JOSH

Who's Mary and Joseph?

GRANDPA

You don't know who Mary and Joseph are?

JOSH

Are they a rap group?

KATIE

Josh. You are sooo embarrassing sometimes.

GRANDPA

I think I need to have a talk with your mother. Anyhow...I'm about to tell you all about Mary and Joseph and the Angels and Magi....

JOSH

...what's a magi? Is that like Star Wars?

KATIE

(Rolling eyes)

Jo..o...o..sh.

GRANDPA

No. They're not like Star Wars. But....they did like stars. Come on, sit down. I'm gonna tell you all about it. Let's see. Where should I begin? It all began when God promised to send the people of the world a messiah. Someone who would save the people of the world from their sins. So they would know who the right person was, he sent special messages through prophets who told us all about the Savior who was to come.

LIGHTS FADE OUT.

<u>SONG</u>

<u>SONG</u>

Scene 4

LIGHTS COME UP.

ISAIAH

(Overdramatic)

Awake, awake, O Zion. This is what the Lord says: To us a child is born, and he will be called Wonderful Counselor, Mighty God, Everlasting Father, Prince of Peace. He shall reign on David's throne and over his kingdom forever and ever. *(Stands still for a moment*) Amen. *(Sighs)* Y'know...I'm a little too old to be doing this. What year is this anyway? *(Choir member responds*) 20_? Well that explains it. I was wonderin' why you all looked so funny. *(Chuckles*) Uh... now...where was I? Oh, yes....name's Isaiah. I'm a prophet by trade. Don't know if you've heard of me but I was pretty well known in my time. Let's see where should I begin. Well...actually I wasn't there for the uh..first Christmas. My part came a few years before that. The way it began was that the Lord came to me in a vision. 'Twas a clear vision, mind you. Just like I can see you here now. Almighty God was on His throne, awesome and powerful. He was surrounded all around by angels who was praisin' Him and singin' "Holy, holy, holy is the Lord". And when I realized that I was in His presence, I was scared as a hare 'cause I knew that I was such a sinner. I was so scared that I cried out, "Lord, I'm unclean". And I was shakin' like a leaf when one of them angels came up and he touched me and he said your guilt is taken away and your sin is erased. At that moment I realized that I had just been forgiven for everything I'd ever done. Boy...it was like ten dozen camels had been lifted off my shoulders. And y'know what? I wasn't scared anymore. Then God spoke and he said, "Whom shall I send? Who will go for us?" So I answered, "Here I am. Send me." So He did. And so what He told me, I told the people of Israel. Y'see God wanted them to repent....to turn around...to come back to Him. But they sure were stubborn. They kept right on sinnin'. But God didn't give up; no way. See...He had a plan. A plan for someone to come to take away all the sin of the world. Someone that would give victory over evil. This person was the Messiah.. the Christ. So I told Israel 'bout this Messiah and 'bout Him being born as a man, and 'bout livin' a life without sin and bringing peace between God and man. Well..it all happened just like God said it would. So....anyhow...my part was tellin' the people about what God had told me...the actual happenin'....that would come later. You'll see what I'm talking about...them angels..they're on their way here this very minute.

LIGHTS FADE OUT.

<u>SONG</u>

Scene 5

LIGHTS COME UP.

SHEPHERD

I remember it just like it was yesterday. Trust me, once you've seen a whole army of angels, that's not something you're likely to forget. The other guys and I were doing the night shift in the hills just outside Bethlehem. Everything was quiet. It was just an ordinary night. One lamb got caught in a bush, and I had to go cut him out, but really other than that, it was as quiet as it could be. Then suddenly there was this THING...this really, really bright thing. He looked like a man, but you could barely look at him because he was so bright. I've...I've never been so scared in my life. I started to run, but he said, "Do not be afraid. I bring you good news of great joy that will be for all the people". Then he told us that a child had just been born, and this child would be the Messiah. The Anointed One. The one who would save the world. I couldn't believe it. He said that we would find this child in the town, a baby wrapped in cloths and lying in a manger. Suddenly, a whole army of bright beings appeared in the sky, an army of angels! They began singing praises to God. My first thought was...well....I've done it now. I've died and gone to heaven. But just as suddenly as they all came, they all disappeared. Well, after all that, you couldn't have held us back with all the horses in Judea. We ran down to Bethlehem, and looked for a manger, and we found the child, and there, just like the angel had described was the most beautiful baby you ever saw. We were so excited. We ran through the town, telling everyone what we'd seen, and praising and glorifying God. What a night! What an amazing night. And I tell you...after that....we were changed men. We would never forget it. And now that I've told you, I hope that you too will be changed and I hope that you won't ever forget it either.

LIGHTS FADE OUT.

<u>SONG</u>

Scene 6

LIGHTS COME UP.

JOSEPH

How shall I begin? Well... it was all very strange. I had always tried to be obedient to the Lord. - just as my father taught me. So naturally I chose my wife, Mary, because she had great faith in the Lord. Of course...it didn't hurt that she was also so beautiful.

MARY

Oh...Joseph. You flatter me so.

JOSEPH

Well it's true. *(To audience)* Let's see....when we became engaged I thought I was the luckiest man in Nazareth. As was the custom, after the engagement, we would not be married for a year. Now, mind you, there were times when it wasn't easy, but I kept my vows. Then one day, like a bolt out of the sky, I found out she was with child. And one thing I knew...the father wasn't me.

MARY

It wasn't an easy time., Joseph and I were just starting to plan our life together. Joseph had a good job - he was a carpenter, and although we didn't have much, we didn't need much. All we really wanted was to live a humble life together, to raise children, and to love and serve the Lord. Everything was going so smoothly....that's when it happened.

I was outside, just having some quiet time, when suddenly this great being appeared. He was so bright that I...I couldn't look at him. But I remember his words exactly; I could never forget. He said, "Don't be afraid. You have found favor with God". Then he said I was going to have a baby. You can imagine my shock.....I was a proper Jewish girl. Before I could begin to understand this, the angel told me that this child, my son, would be named Jesus, and would be called the Son of God, and that he would inherit the throne of David. He said His kingdom would be forever. As you can imagine, I....I didn't know what to think. All I could say was, "How can this be...I have never been with a man?" And he answered, "Nothing is impossible with God."

JOSEPH

When, Mary told me that she was having the child, I didn't know what to do. It was hard to believe such a story. But, I didn't want to divorce her. As much as it hurt, I still loved her. After thinking about it for awhile, I decided that I would do it privately. That way there would be no public disgrace. But then I had the dream. In the dream the angel said, "Don't be afraid to take Mary home as your wife, for what is conceived in her is from the Holy Spirit". He also said, "She will give birth to a son, and you are to give Him the name Jesus." I'm not sure I was totally convinced, but I trusted God and I took Mary to be my wife.

MARY

It all happened just as the angel said. I became with child and gave birth to a son. The circumstances weren't the best, mind you, and for awhile I began to wonder if this angel had just been a dream. But after His birth, my doubts were washed away by the many wonders and signs which God provided. I treasured these things in my heart and I know that even though He was my son, He was truly God's son. You know it was only much later, after His terrible death.... on that cross....that I began to realize what it all fully meant. You see, even though I gave Jesus life here on earth, it is He who gave me a life...a life which is eternal, a life in the presence of God. And that is the best gift of all.

MARY goes to get baby from offstage, and then returns holding the child.

JOSEPH

I often thought about the name the angel told us to give Him. Jesus...that means Savior. Why would God want us to put such a heavy burden on a little child? But according to the angel, this was all part of God's plan, just like the prophet Isaiah had said. Later on I learned that Jesus was the one we call IMMANUEL"....which means "God with us". "IMMANUEL"...God with us....."IMMANUEL"...God with us.....and then I finally understood it. I got it! With the birth of this child....Jesus...God WAS with us!

LIGHTS FADE OUT.

<u>SONG</u>

<u>SONG</u>

Scene 7

LIGHTS COME UP.

MAGI

Y'know, I never do get tired of looking at the stars. For me the stars are...well, like friends. I knew them pretty well...still do. Whenever a new star appeared in the sky, my colleagues and I would study it with fascination, wondering what it might do, or what it might portend. The star I'm about to tell you about was unlike any other I have ever seen. It arose in the Western sky quite suddenly.... in one night. It was so bright that you could see it in the daytime. But what was most strange was... it didn't move. It appeared to be quite stationary over one spot, off in the distance in the direction of Jerusalem. We knew something significant had happened, but we weren't sure what it was. Someone said that it might have something to do with the prophecies about a new king who would appear over Israel. There was much debate until, finally, we decided that we must know. So we began a journey to follow this star. As we traveled, the star seemed to go on before us, always on before us, until at last we arrived in a little town called Bethlehem, not far from Jerusalem. There the star led us to the place where a child was, and there the star stopped. When we saw this child, and his mother and his father, we were filled with great joy. Then we bowed down to worship him for though he was just a babe, he was truly a King. And as a King, we presented him with gifts of gold, incense, and myrrh. It's hard to explain, but I was overcome with the sense that somehow....God was very near. I did not learn the full meaning of the life of this child for many years. You see, this child, born with such humble beginnings, gave me a gift, the gift of life eternal, a gift given so freely that anyone might accept it. All I had to do was accept it. My prayer is that you too, will accept this gift. Peace be with you.

LIGHTS FADE OUT.

<u>SONG</u>

<u>SONG</u>

Scene 8

LIGHTS COME UP.

GRANDPA and the KIDS are bustling around putting the finishing touches on Christmas decorations for the living room.

GRANDPA

How you doin' over there Josh? Your mother should be home in less than 10 minutes.

KATIE

(Holding cell phone)

She just texted me. She's on her way home now.

GRANDPA

Okay. Kiddos. What's left to do?

KATIE

This is the last piece of garland for the tree.

GRANDPA

All we need now are some presents, right-o Josh?

JOSH

(Non-committal)

Yeah. I guess so.

GRANDPA

Whad' ya mean, you guess so?

JOSH

Well I feel kinda bad now, Grandpa.

GRANDPA

You feel bad? Why son?

JOSH

Because all I wanted out of Christmas was a bunch of gifts and stuff.

GRANDPA

Ah, I see. Son come over here. There's nothing wrong with receiving gifts. After all, the most important thing in the world is a gift: God's gift....Jesus. And God certainly hopes that we will accept His gift.

KATIE

Wow, Grandpa, I never thought of it that way.

GRANDPA

Well I didn't either when I was your age. And you know what? As you both grow a little older, you will find out that there can be just as much joy in giving a gift, as in receiving one.

JOSH

Really? As much fun as getting one?

GRANDPA

Yep.

KATIE

Grandpa, do you think maybe God feels that way about giving us His gift too?

GRANDPA

You mean it being as much fun giving a gift as receiving one?

KATIE

Yeah.

GRANDPA

Well I never thought of it that way. But now that I do, I would think He does. You're a smart girl, Katie.

GRANDPA and KATIE exchange hugs.

JOSH

Maybe I can make my wish list fit on one page.

KATIE

Now that's what I call progress.

MARGIE ENTERS.

MARGIE

Oh, will you look at that!. What have you all been doing here?

KATIE and JOSH

(Holding out arms)

TA-DA! Merry Christmas!

MARGIE

I can't believe you guys did all this.

JOSH

It was fun.

KATIE

Yeah and we made cookies too. I'll get you some.

KATIE EXITS.

LARRY ENTERS.

LARRY

Hi everyone, I'm home. *(Pauses)* Hey, nice tree!

MARGIE

Yeah. Isn't it great!

KATIE REENTERS with COOKIES. She hands one to both MARGIE and LARRY.

MARGIE

Mmn. These are good. Just like the ones Mom used to make.

LARRY

She's right. These ARE good!

MARGIE

Dad. I'm so proud of you. All you ever made for us was soup.

GRANDPA

Well I couldn't live with your mother all those years without picking up a trick or two. Besides Josh and Katie did most of the work.

GRANDPA hugs MARGIE.

JOSH

Grandpa...do you miss Grandma?

MARGIE

Josh!

GRANDPA

It's okay. Of course I do Josh. But you know what really helps me? It's the fact that I know that she accepted God's gift and that I have too. And so I know that now she's in heaven in a room that God prepared just for her and someday, when my time comes and I leave this earth, I know that I'll be right there with her.

MARGIE

Dad...that's beautiful.

LARRY

(Walks over and pats GRANDPA on the back)

JOSH

I'm hungry

GRANDPA

What? You didn't eat enough cookies?

JOSH

Nope.

LARRY

We thought we'd treat you out to dinner tonight? Is that all right?

GRANDPA

Larry, I learned something a long time ago. Never turn down a free dinner.

LARRY

All right then. Well...uh...let's go. *(To Margie)* My car or yours?

MARGIE

Remember, mine's a mess.

LARRY

Oh, yeah. Well...we'll take mine. Let's head on out. Bill, you like Carrabbas?

ALL start heading to the EXIT.

GRANDPA

That's one of my favorites.

LARRY

Good. That's where we're headed.

GRANDPA

Right-o.

LARRY EXITS.

MARGIE

Dad, thank you. It's starting to feel like Christmas.

KATIE and JOSH

Yay. It's starting to feel like Christmas.

GRANDPA

Well... a Happy Christmas to all and to all a good night.

JOSH

What?

KATIE

It's from a famous poem silly.

GRANDPA

Margie. I think I need to talk to you about that boy.

MARGIE

Dad..let's not get started.

ALL EXIT.

JOSH REENTERS.

JOSH

(Yelling back to the others)

I forgot my Itunes.

JOSH runs over to the sofa, picks up his itune player, and rushes back to the EXIT.

JOSH

(From offstage)

Hey, don't leave without me!

LIGHTS FADE OUT.

MESSAGE

<u>SONG</u>

Wise Men Still Seek Him

By Skip Martin

<u>OVERTURE</u>

<u>SONG</u>

Scene 1

LIGHTS COME UP

SHANNON

Mom...MOM.

BEVERLY

(From offstage)

Shannon I'm trying to get ready. You're going to have to come back here.

SHANNON

(Sighing)

Mom. I can't find my vanity mirror.

KEVIN

What's the matter...can't stare at yourself?

SHANNON

You know. One of these days you're going to turn from a little tadpole into a frog. By the way there's a pimple on your left nostril.

KEVIN

Where? *(Pulls a small vanity mirror from the back of his pants)*

SHANNON

Give me that!

SHANNON reaches for the mirror and a small tussle erupts just as BEVERLY enters from stage left.

BEVERLY

Stop that right this instant!

KEVIN relinquishes the mirror as SHANNON stalks away indignantly.

BEVERLY

You both should be ashamed of yourselves. It's Christmas Eve and you're behaving like...ragamuffins.

SHANNON

But he took my mirror.

KEVIN

She said I had a pimple.

SHANNON

You are a pimple.

BEVERLY

I said that's enough. I want you to listen to me. Grandpa's going to watch you while I finish shopping. Do you think you can behave yourselves while I'm gone?

BOTH CHILDREN

(Reluctantly)

Yes.

BEVERLY

By the way. Where is Grandpa?

SHANNON

He's upstairs with Carrie.

BEVERLY

Carrie. Where are you?

CARRIE

(From offstage upstairs)

Here, mom.

BEVERLY

What are you guys doing up there?

CARRIE enters from upstairs. Stage left.

CARRIE

Grandpa's showing me how to use the telescope. It's really neat.

GRANDPA enters from upstairs. Stage left.

GRANDPA

Righto. I think we have the makings of a young astronomer here.

BEVERLY

Dad. I'm about to go. I should be back in about two hours. Then I've got reservations at Chequers.. So, do you think you all can be ready?

GRANDPA

We're going to eat Christmas dinner at a drive-through?

BEVERLY

That's Chequers with a q Dad. Trust me. It's a very nice place. You'll like it.

GRANDPA

What about Christmas eve service?

BEVERLY

Dad...please...don't start with me. It's just...not practical. Not with these kids.

GRANDPA

Fiddlesticks. If you don't celebrate Christmas in church. Then...you're not celebrating Christmas.

BEVERLY

Dad. I know. But things are different now. We can't always do things the way we used to. Look...Dad...I've gotta go. Let's discuss this when I get back.

GRANDPA

Well...you go on and go. We'll be just fine. *(Motions to her)* Go on.

BEVERLY

Thanks. I want you guys to cooperate with Grandpa. Y'hear. And be dressed and ready to go when I get back.

CHILDREN

Yes, mom.

BEVERLY

Bye.

BEVERLY EXITS.

GRANDPA

Okay. The coast is clear. Now we can have some fun. Who wants to use the telescope?

SHANNON

Not me. I'm going to go watch Netflix.

SHANNON exits stage left.

KEVIN

No thanks Gramps. I'm going to play with my *(latest popular computer game).*

KEVIN exits stage right.

GRANDPA

What's *(latest popular computer game)*?

CARRIE

That's a computer game Grandpa. I don't know how anyone can spend so much time on such silly games? Well, I guess its just you and me.

GRANDPA

All right, after me my dear Alphonso.

CARRIE

No. After me, my dear Alphonso.

LIGHTS FADE OUT.

<u>SONG</u>

Scene 2

LIGHTS COME UP.

GRANDPA and CARRIE are on the balcony. CARRIE is peering through a telescope while GRANDPA assists.

GRANDPA

Can you see it now?

CARRIE

No. Not yet.

GRANDPA

Here. Let me try it.

GRANDPA takes over and peers through the lens, making a few adjustments.

GRANDPA

Ah, there. Now try it.

CARRIE

Neato.

GRANDPA

Yes. Isn't it? That's Grandpa's favorite. Hey, look...quick there's a shooting star.

CARRIE

(Excitedly)

I saw it, I saw it. Up close and big. It had flames and everything.

KEVIN and SHANNON come running in.

KEVIN

What's going on?

SHANNON

What's all that noise?

CARRIE

I just saw a shooting star. It was really cool.

GRANDPA

Astronomers call it a comet.

SHANNON

You mean like Haley's comet?

GRANDPA

Yes. In a way.

KEVIN

Let me look.

SHANNON

It's gone now, silly.

KEVIN

(Peering through eyepiece)

Grandpa will it come back?

GRANDPA

Not that one I'm afraid.

KEVIN

Aw, every time something exciting happens I miss it.

CARRIE

Grandpa you know that star that was with baby Jesus. Was that a comet?

GRANDPA

I don't think so.

CARRIE

What was it then?

GRANDPA

You know, a long time ago, a couple of fellows asked themselves that very question. They lived in a country far away in the east. This was before we had Christmas.

KEVIN

Before Christmas? Bummer. How could the kids get presents?

GRANDPA

Well they had other celebrations.

KEVIN

What did they celebrate?

GRANDPA

Oh they celebrated the usual things: the sun, the rain, the time of harvest. You see they knew that they were dependant upon the elements...for their daily food. They studied the stars hoping for a sign that would help them in their struggle for day to day existence. Some of these men were very educated in their studies. They kept charts of the skies. They knew when to expect to see the constellations and planets at the proper place in the sky.

SHANNON

Wow, I didn't know they knew all that stuff.

GRANDPA

Oh, they were quite knowledgeable. They were called Magi. You know how they talk about the three kings who brought gifts to the baby Jesus? Those men were Magi.

KEVIN

Grandpa, how do you know all this stuff?

GRANDPA

Well, let's just say that I picked up a few things over the years. Tell you what I'm gonna do. I'm gonna tell you a story about the Magi. Everyone take a seat.

THE CHILDREN gather around GRANDPA. As the story begins the lights slowly fade out.

Now. A long time ago in a country far to the east of the land we now call Israel, lived a group of Magi. They're names were Balthasar, Melchior, and Caspar. And they spent all of the spare time they had studying the stars....

THE LIGHTS FADE DOWN as GRANDPA tells the story.

SONG

SONG

SONG

SONG

Scene 3

LIGHTS COME UP.

BALTHASAR enters upper stage right. It is night. He is standing on a rooftop studying the stars.

BALTHASAR

Star light..star bright...how are all my friends tonight? Good evening Mr. Ram. Hello, Mr. Bull...oh, and you Capricornus. Ah...it is so good to see you all. Hello? What's this? I haven't seen you before. Hmm. Melchior...we're not expecting any visitors in the region of Cepheus tonight are we?

MELCHIOR

(From offstage)

Visitors? Oh, no. Please don't tell me its another one of those noisy and smelly caravans.

BALTHASAR

No..no. I'm talking about a star. You might want to come and take a look at it. I haven't seen this one before. Its quite unusual. *(There is a pause)* MELCHIOR, you must come and see this.

MELCHIOR

All right...all right. This better not be one your jokes. Where is it?

BALTHASAR

There. Twenty degrees above the horizon.

MELCHIOR

Good heavens.

BALTHASAR

Can't you be a little more original?

MELCHIOR

(Glaring)

Don't start with me. All right...so it's a bright star. What of it? I'm sure that the prophets have observed it before.

BALTHASAR

No. I'm quite sure that I have read nothing about this star.

MELCHIOR

Then, what do you think? This is some sign from the gods? I'll wager you that Caspar could tell us all about it.

BALTHASAR

Whether it is a sign from a god I do not know, but I do know that this star has not been written of before. This is a new star.

MELCHIOR

New star? Come now. You can't be serious. *(Pauses)* You are serious. Look, there's one way that we can settle this. Let's go see Caspar. If it's been seen before he will have it among his scrolls.

BALTHASAR

All right then, let's go.

THE MEN exit stage right.

LIGHTS FADE OUT

<u>SONG</u>

Scene 4

THE STAGE LIGHTS come on as we see BALTHASAR, MELCHIOR, and CASPAR, seated amidst sets of scrolls scattered in disarray.

BALTHASAR

Is there any that we have missed?

CASPAR

(Thoughtfully)

No. We've gone through all the Egyptian...the Phoenician...the Greek. I think we've covered them all.

MELCHIOR

Isn't there something we've missed?

CASPAR shakes head silently and then walks over to extend his arms to BALTHASAR.

CASPAR

Congratulations. Balthasar, I think you have discovered a new star.

BALTHASAR grins knowingly at MELCHIOR who waves him off.

CASPAR

The question is what does it mean?

MELCHIOR

Does it have to mean anything? Can't it just be a new star?

CASPAR

Yes, it can. But we know from the past that a new star can be a sign. A very important sign.

BALTHASAR

A star this bright...appearing so suddenly. It must be a sign of something significant. I don't know...maybe an important birth? Maybe a new king?

CASPAR

I have read of a prophecy about the birth of new king.

BALTHASAR

Well? What is it? Tell us about it.

CASPAR

It was written by the prophet, Isaiah, and it speaks of a ruler who will be righteous and just and will reign on David's throne and David's kingdom.

BALTHASAR

Does it say for how long?

CASPAR

It says forever.

MELCHIOR

Yes. And a camel can go through the eye of a needle.

CASPAR

You speak as if you have eaten bitter fruit, my friend. Don't you ever think about the deeper things? Have you not ever wondered why we even exist, you and I? Is life nothing but a vanity?

MELCHIOR

I think that what you see is what you get. That's what I think.

BALTHASAR

Come now my friends. You said the prophecy speaks of David's kingdom. Would that not be the David who was king of Israel?

CASPAR

Yes, I believe that is the one.

MELCHIOR

He was the father of Solomon who was the wealthiest king in the world. Married the Pharaoh's daughter and courted the queen of Sheba. He was known throughout the world for his great wisdom...and his seven hundred wives. *(Pauses)* That part doesn't sound so smart to me.

The other two look at MELCHIOR in amazement.

MELCHIOR

What? I do read you know.

BALTHASAR

Well then, the land is now called Judea. If there is a new king of such greatness, then we would do well to go and do him honor.

MELCHIOR

That would be a journey of a thousand miles!

CASPAR

We should take gifts fit for a king.

BALTHASAR

Gold fit for king.

CASPAR

Incense for one who is righteous and pure.

MELCHIOR

And myrrh for his burial. *(Shrugs)* No one lives forever.

BALTHASAR

So you will come?

MELCHIOR

Even if there were such a King, how would we even find him?

BALTHASAR AND CASPAR

Follow the Star.

BALTHASAR

Are you with us?

MELCHIOR

Okay. All right, I know when I'm beaten.

CASPAR

There is a caravan headed west, the day after tomorrow. Let us join with them.

LIGHTS FADE OUT.

<u>SONG</u>

Scene 5

LIGHTS COME UP.

IT IS NIGHT in the desert. BALTHASAR and CASPAR are arranging their bedding. MELCHIOR ENTERS from lower stage right carrying his gear.

MELCHIOR

If I ride that camel another cubit I think I'm going to die. *(Puts down his bedding and then groans)* That does it.

BALTHASAR

Cheer up, Melchior. I was talking to the camel master. We should be there in just three more weeks.

MELCHIOR

(Groaning)

Why doesn't that cheer me up?

BALTHASAR

Look up in the sky. The star has been going before us every step of the way.

CASPAR

It defies reason. Nothing can explain it.

MELCHIOR

I must admit that I've never seen anything like it. But I'm sure there is an answer. That is what keeps me going.

BALTHASAR

You know on a night like this, with all the stars spread out before us, splendid in their majesty, you can't help but wonder about the meaning of it all. How did they get created? Why are they so orderly and consistent? Then you wonder: did whatever being that created them, also create us? Why are we here? And what will happen to us when we die?

CASPAR

I was talking to one of the traders who is a Jew. They believe in one God who created all things.

BALTHASAR

Yes. I hear that they are waiting for a messiah who will bring them their freedom.

MELCHIOR

He will have to bring many legions with him, for I think that the Romans may want to have something to say about that.

CASPAR

Maybe that is not the kind of freedom they speak of?

MELCHIOR

What other kind of freedom is there?

CASPAR

Freedom from all the worries and burdens of this life. Freedom from injustice. Freedom from the evil that men do to each other.

MELCHIOR

Yes. That would be a sweet freedom.

BALTHASAR

This star...there is something about this star. It is not like an ordinary star. It is not like one of the wanderers that we know. It's...it's practically leading us someplace as if...by a tether.

MELCHIOR

It's quite obvious that it's leading us to Jerusalem.

CASPAR

Yes. The seat of David's kingdom. How interesting.

MELCHIOR

Still thinking about the king whose kingdom will reign forever?

CASPAR

Yes. What kind of king could that be? Surely, no mere mortal or man.

MELCHIOR

Perhaps a god then.

BALTHASAR

But you think not?

MELCHIOR

(Chuckling)

I have learned to put my faith in solid things. Things I can test to see if they are true. Things like stars I can know and can study.

BALTHASAR

What about this star? The one we have been following.

MELCHIOR

I'm sure there is a logical explanation for it.

CASPAR

Do you not think that there is a God?

MELCHIOR

If there is a God I wish he would come down from his perch in the heavens, and answer some of the questions I have for him. Why doesn't he speak to us? Why does he allow an innocent child to die? Why does he allow such men as those from Rome to rule this world?

BALTHASAR

Maybe it is like the ants?

CASPAR

How do you mean?

BALTHASAR

If I approach a hill of ants, to watch them, to study what they are doing, they become terrified. They scurry around in every direction. If I could talk to them, explain things that they don't understand, then they would not be afraid, they would understand. But I cannot do that because I am a man, and they are ants.

In order to truly talk to them, I would have to become like them, and become one of them. I would have to become an ant.

MELCHIOR

The only problem is, you can't be an ant.

BALTHASAR

If I were God I could.

MELCHIOR

Ah...my friend. You are quick with speech, like a centurion with sword. Soon you will have me believe that we are part of a divine plan.

CASPAR

With this star, who is to say we are not?

LIGHTS FADE OUT.

<u>SONG</u>

<u>SONG</u>

Scene 7

LIGHTS COME UP.

NIGHTTIME in the desert.

BALTHASAR

The star is almost overhead now.

CASPAR

We must be close.

MELCHIOR

I hope so. The closer we get to Jerusalem the wilder the stories get. Today I heard a tale of shepherds seeing a multitude of angels in the hills near the city. Can you believe that?

CASPAR

Why did you not tell us?

MELCHIOR

I do not believe in such spirits. Besides, I was busy looking over my shoulder for Herod's henchmen.

BALTHASAR

Yes. He did not seem happy to learn of the birth of a new king.

CASPAR

It doesn't make any sense? How could he not know?

MELCHIOR

This whole thing doesn't make any sense to me.

BALTHASAR

At least the priests knew of the prophecy.

CASPAR

Yes. That is true.

BALTHASAR

And that the King's birth would be in Bethlehem, which can't be much further.

CASPAR

Look! It has stopped.

BALTHASAR

I think you are right.

MELCHIOR

Now what?

CASPAR

Maybe this would be a good time for faith?

MELCHIOR

Faith in what?

BALTHASAR

Faith that there is something greater than ourselves.

MELCHIOR

Where is the King? There is no palace here.

BALTHASAR

Perhaps it not the type of king you expect? *(Pauses)* Look! The star is shining there!

CASPAR

Shall we go there?

MELCHIOR

Is this the end of our journey?

CASPAR

Perhaps it is only the beginning.

LIGHTS FADE OUT.

<u>SONG</u>

<u>SONG</u>

Scene 8

LIGHTS COME UP.

GRANDPA is seated in his stuffed chair with CARRIE and SHANNON sitting at his feet listening raptly. KEVIN is standing by the telescope.

SHANNON

That was a pretty neat story Grandpa. How come I never knew any of that stuff?

GRANDPA

How could you know if no one ever told you?

KEVIN

Grandpa, I don't get it? If baby Jesus was God, how come he died like he did? Wasn't he supposed to live forever?

GRANDPA

Well...you see...Jesus becoming a man to show us what God was like was only part of God's plan. By living among us and teaching us, Jesus showed us what God was like. But that doesn't solve the problem of sin.

SHANNON

How come? Can't God just...like...forgive us?

GRANDPA

Well, you see, there is another part of God. He is perfect and Holy. To live in his presence we must be free of sin because God absolutely cannot tolerate sin. I'll make you a bet...I'll bet you can't give me the name of one person who is perfect...that never did one bad thing in their whole life.

SHANNON

Hmm...well its definitely not Madonna. That's for sure. I dunno. I guess there isn't anyone.

GRANDPA

Ah, that was God's problem. No one could live in God's presence because no one is without sin. If you tried to make things right with God by doing something, by not sinning again, you would always fail, because no matter how hard you tried you cannot live a perfect life. It's impossible. That's where Jesus comes in. Jesus by His life of perfect obedience, and death of love, gave up His life as the one and only sacrifice to God that completely wipes the slate clean.

SHANNON

How do we know that?

GRANDPA

Well...after the visit from the Magi, Jesus grew up. Then for three years He walked the land, teaching us about God and telling us how much God loves us. So that we could understand God, He often told stories, which are called parables. One of them is kind of like this: suppose that one day, on the way home from school, you got lost and didn't come home. What do you think your Mom would do?

SHANNON

Oh, man. She'd freak out. She'd go looking for me everywhere.

GRANDPA

Yes, your Mom loves you a lot. Well, according to Jesus, that's the kind of love God has for you, too. Jesus came to tell us, bad as we are, that God still loves us. So when we turn away from God and are lost, He searches everywhere for us - just like your Mom would. Jesus came to tell us that though we are sinners, we are still dear to God. Our part of the deal is that we have to trust Jesus and when we do that, it changes our whole relationship with God. If we believe in Jesus, God accepts us and forgives us.

KEVIN

I get it. I think I actually get it!

CARRIE

I feel bad Grandpa.

GRANDPA

Why, Carrie?

CARRIE

Because Christmas is Jesus birthday, and we didn't give Him a present.

GRANDPA

Hmm. I have an idea about what the best present we can give Jesus might be?

CHILDREN

What?

GRANDPA

To go to His house and thank Him for everything He has done for us.

KEVIN

You mean go to Church?

GRANDPA nods.

SHANNON

Let's do it.

CARRIE

This will be the best Christmas ever.

KEVIN

(To Shannon)

I'm sorry I took your mirror.

SHANNON

That's okay. *(She hugs her brother)*

BEVERLY returns from shopping, entering stage left.

BEVERLY

Well it looks like the Christmas spirit must be catching.

CARRIE

Mom..guess what? We know all about the Magi, and the star and the three gifts.

KEVIN

Yeah. And we want to go to the Christmas Eve service. Can we please?

BEVERLY

Are you okay? Should I take your temperature?

SHANNON

Mom. We mean it.

BEVERLY

What about dinner, and your presents?

KEVIN

We can eat dinner any ole time, but how often can we honor a King on His birthday?

BEVERLY

All right, Dad. What did you do? These are not the same kids I had earlier today.

GRANDPA

Beverly. It's the spirit of Christmas.

CARRIE

Look Grandpa, there's the star you where talking about.

GRANDPA

The star?

CARRIE

You know the star that the wise men followed. There it is.

THE WHOLE FAMILY crowds around trying to get a glimpse out the window.

SHANNON and KEVIN

I see it. I see it.

GRANDPA

Remarkable.

CARRIE

Grandpa, is that the same star you told us about?

GRANDPA

I don't know. I've never seen that one before. *(Pauses)* Beverly, isn't that the direction to First Baptist Church?

BEVERLY

As a matter of fact, I think it is.

GRANDPA

There's only one way to find out. Let's follow the star.

CHILDREN

Hooray. Let's go.

BEVERLY

All right. All right I know when I'm beaten.

EVERYONE gathers up their coats and begin to head out the door. GRANDPA lags behind and stops to look out the window one more time. CARRIE waits in the doorway, watching GRANDPA.

GRANDPA

(Appearing to talk to himself)

This is very unusual. I haven't seen this star before. You might want to come and take a look at it. *(There is a pause)* Where's Melchior when you need him.?

CARRIE

Grandpa...how old are you?

LIGHTS FADE OUT.

MESSAGE

SONG

SONG

Where's The Line For Jesus?

By Skip Martin

<u>OVERTURE</u>

Scene 1

LIGHTS COME UP.

LISA AND ETHAN ENTER from the stage left hallway as they walk into the MAIN STREET MALL. SANTA CLAUS is seated in a chair on stage right with a long line of children and their parents waiting for their turn to talk to SANTA.

LISA

Ethan! We'd better hurry. I don't know how much longer he'll be here.

LISA anxiously tries to see around the corner.

LISA

Oh, good. He's still here. C'mon. You don't want to miss him.

ETHAN

(Less than thrilled)

That's okay Mom. I think I'll survive.

LISA

I can't believe that you don't want to see Santa Claus. What's the matter with you?

ETHAN

Mom. Don't you think I'm a little too old for this?

LISA

Old? You? You're not too old for Santa. You're only 9!

ETHAN

But Mom, I stopped believing in Santa Claus when I was in first grade. Remember? I saw Dad sneaking that bicycle from Santa into the utility room.

LISA

Well...that was just Daddy helping Santa...nevermind. You're still not too old to visit with Santa. Besides I have to get a picture of you with Santa for the Christmas Card this year. This may be the last year that I can do this. C'mon.

ETHAN

(Sighing)

Okay.

ETHAN reluctantly follows LISA to the end of the line for Santa. As he slowly walks he curiously looks around.

ETHAN

Mom, I wanna ask you something.

LISA

Yes, honey?

ETHAN

Mom, I wanna ask you something,

LISA

Yes, dear. Go ahead.

ETHAN

Momma, you gotta listen.

LISA

Ethan, what has gotten into you? What is it?

ETHAN

How come He doesn't have a line?

LISA

Who dear? Who are you talking about?

ETHAN

You know. Jesus. Where's the line for Jesus?

LISA

(Stunned)

Where's the line for Jesus? I uh...uh...I don't. know.

LIGHTS FADE OUT.

<u>SONG</u>

Scene 2

LIGHTS COME UP to reveal the HOWE LIVING ROOM. LISA and RICHARD are standing in the middle of the room.

LISA

....and just out of the middle of nowhere he just asks me this question, "Where's the line for Jesus"?

RICHARD

"Where's the line for Jesus?"

LISA

Yes. "Where's the line for Jesus".

RICHARD

Where did he get that from?

LISA

I have no idea. I was hoping you might know,.

RICHARD

I have no idea. That's very strange.

LISA

Yes. And in the middle of the mall. Of all places.

RICHARD

Well...at least it wasn't in church.

LISA

That's not very funny.

RICHARD

Okay. Seriously. Where do you think he got that from? I don't think he got it from one of us.

LISA

No. Probably not.

RICHARD

Well he must have gotten it from somewhere.

LISA

Wait a minute. I have an idea.

RICHARD

What?

LISA

Well...he has been spending a lot of time next door playing with his friend Thomas.

RICHARD

You mean next door with the religious nuts?

LISA

Richard, just because they go to church every Sunday doesn't make them religious nuts.

RICHARD

Yeah, but who does that anymore?

LISA

But that still doesn't make them nuts.

RICHARD

Okay, whatever.

LISA

Maybe we can invite them over so we find out what they're up to?

RICHARD

You're serious?

LISA

Yes. This is something that involves our son and I want to find out what's going on.

RICHARD

You are serious.

LISA

I am. I've got an idea. Here's what we can do. We can invite them over and just sort of start a conversation about spiritual stuff...y'know to get them talking. Then maybe we can find out what's happened to Ethan?

RICHARD

Yes...I see what you're saying. That might work.

LISA

Yeah. They're bound to start talking all about church because y'know they might think they can convert us or something.

RICHARD

Not much chance of that.

LISA

Yeah, but they don't know that.

RICHARD

Okay. All right. I'll agree to this. But I just wanna say one thing - there will definitely be no lines for Jesus in our house.

LIGHT FADE OUT.

<u>SONG</u>

Scene 3

LIGHTS COME UP to reveal the SCOTT LIVING ROM. LUKE and JULIE are standing in the middle of the room.

LUKE

She just invited us over, huh?

JULIE

Yeah. Isn't that great?

LUKE

Well, it's about time. Y'know we haven't been over to their house one single time and it's been nearly three years since we moved in...right?

JULIE

Actually it's been a little more like four...cuz Thomas was four when we moved here and now he's eight.

LUKE

Wonder why? Y'know just all of the sudden they just invite us over? Hey, maybe we can invite them to church?

JULIE

I don't know. Let's make a pact. Let's not push God on them. I don't want to seem overbearing and scare them away, y'know? Let's just get to know them, see if we can develop a friendship, and then maybe later on, we can bring up spiritual things.

LUKE

Okay. Sounds good to me. We won't bring up church...or Jesus...

JULIE

..or God....or faith...or anything spiritual.

LUKE

Deal. All we're gonna do is just try to get to know them

JULIE

You got it!.

THE SCOTTS shake hands.

LIGHTS FADE OUT.

<u>SONG</u>

<u>SONG</u>

Scene 4

LIGHTS COME UP to reveal the HOWE LIVING ROOM.

LUKE

We really appreciate you inviting us over Richard.

RICHARD

Well actually....Lisa deserves the credit for that. It was her idea.

JULIE

Well, thank you Lisa. I've been telling Luke for some time that we really need to get to know our neighbors a little better.

LISA

Yes. Absolutely. We feel exactly the same way. Say...did you guys notice that new church they're building up the road? I really hope it's one of those cute ones with the steeple and everything. Y'know we don't go to church ourselves but I kinda think that spiritual stuff can be fascinating, don't you?

LUKE and JULIE look at each other and then begin nodding.

LUKE

Um...sure.

RICHARD

Did you guys see that article in the paper today? The one about the lawsuit involving a church? Y'know just because of some bad apples, people forget all the good things that the church has done for people. I mean they feed the homeless and visit sick people. I don't believe in God but I'm glad that there are some religious people doing some good stuff in the world. I think that's a good thing, don't you?

LUKE and JULIE look at each other and then begin nodding again.

LUKE

Um...yeah. We do too.

LISA

I have to tell you...Ethan really enjoys going to church with Thomas.

JULIE

(Looking at LUKE)

Well I'm glad to hear that.

RICHARD

Actually I'm glad you brought that up...church, that is.

JULIE

(Giving another questioning look to LUKE)

Really? Did you have some questions about...church?

RICHARD

Er...uh...as a matter of fact I did.

JULIE

(Gives yet another questioning look to LUKE who nods back)

Sure. Go ahead. Ask us anything you want.

RICHARD

Well...just uh...exactly what do you have the kids do there? Sit around and sing Kum By Yah?

JULIE and LUKE

(Chuckling)

I don't think they've ever done that. Usually all the kids get together in one room and they start off by playing some type of game or two to break the ice, and then y'know they break out into smaller groups for some time of fellowship and discussion.

RICHARD

Oh, fellowship? I see. And uh....what sort of things do they talk about in fellowship and discussion?

LUKE

Well actually...at that age we usually just lead a discussion about some important principle like how it's always important to honor your father and mother.

LISA

Well...that sounds revolutionary.

JULIE

Today it almost is. For many of the kids who come...they just have no concept of that.

RICHARD

Well that doesn't sound so bad. So when do you hit them over the head with the Bible?

LISA

Richard!

LUKE

That's okay. We know what you mean. Here's the thing you need to understand. At our church we believe very strongly in the concept of free will. The whole problem with sin, of course, is that God didn't make us robots. So we were created with the ability to choose....to obey Him or not to obey Him. So yes, we believe and teach that what the Bible says is true, but each person has to make their own decision.

RICHARD

So I'm totally free to disregard the Bible and do whatever I want?.

LUKE

Yes, you are.

RICHARD

Well, good. That's what I intend to do. You know I think the church is great. You people do good things and everything. But I just don't believe in Jesus. If it was up to me I'd just as soon celebrate Christmas and leave Jesus out of it.

JULIE

But Richard, if you took Christ out of Christmas, then all you'd have is 'Mas.

LISA

Just 'Mas?

RICHARD

Very well then that's it. Merry 'Mas everyone.

LIGHTS FADE OUT.

<u>SONG</u>

Scene 5

LIGHTS COME UP to reveal the SCOTT LIVING ROOM.

LISA

I have a confession to make. When we invited you guys over the other day, I was trying to find out about what Ethan was being exposed to over at your church. Because he said something really funny to me the other day and I was just trying to find out what was going on.

JULIE

Oh. I see.

LISA

You see. We were at the mall and there was this big long line for Santa Claus and then out of the blue he says to me, "Mom. Where's the line for Jesus?"

JULIE

Really? "Where's the line for Jesus?"

LISA

Yeah. So, I'm like. Where did that come from?

JULIE

So you were worried that...somehow our church may have brainwashed your child?

LISA

No. Yes. Maybe.

JULIE

Lisa, let me assure you of one thing. As a Christian, what I believe and what we believe as a church is that faith cannot be forced on anyone. It's a matter of choice. Each person must accept God or reject God completely on their own. He does not force himself on anyone. One way I've heard it explained is that Jesus knocks, but He always waits for you to open the door.

LISA

I see. Can I ask you a question?

JULIE

Sure. Go ahead.

LISA

Why do you people think that I or anyone needs Jesus anyway?

JULIE

Lisa, have you ever done anything wrong? I mean in your whole life: have you ever done anything bad? Y'now...that you really knew was wrong?

LISA

Oh, Lord....yes.

JULIE

Well. Did you deserve to get punished?

LISA

Yeah. Sure...I guess.

JULIE

Well wouldn't you like to have a pardon so that you wouldn't have to take that punishment?

LISA

I guess. But I'm not sure what you mean?

JULIE

That need for a pardon is why we need Jesus. You see God is perfect and He has perfect standards, one of which is perfect justice. When we've done something wrong, that's called sin. And if God's perfect standard of justice is perfect, then there must be a punishment. That punishment is eternal death; because with our sin we can never be in the presence of God. But you see... God is also a God of mercy and grace. So He has provided a way out. That way out is Jesus. When Jesus died on the cross, He died in our place in order to take our punishment. He is our pardon.

LISA

What if somebody doesn't believe that?

JULIE

Well remember, God never forces us. So...if we don't want to receive the pardon, we can freely choose not to accept it and then...face the consequences that follow.

LISA

And what is that?

JULIE

Well there is a place where there will be people that have decided that they don't want to be with God. The Bible calls that place Hell.

LISA

Oh. *(Pauses)* That part about accepting the pardon does sound good. But how do you do that?

JULIE

Look, let me show you. Here's a gift. If someone gave you a gift wouldn't you want to accept it?

LISA

Sure, I guess.

JULIE

That's all you do. You simply say a little prayer to God that asks for forgiveness for the things you've done wrong, and then you say to Him, "Yes. I accept Jesus, as your pardon for my sins" and now I want to turn away from a life of rejecting you, and begin a new life of following you.

LISA

That sounds so simple

JULIE

Exactly. God's plan has to be simple so that anyone can understand it. You see... He is also a God of Love and He wants everyone whom he has created to be with Him forever. *(Pauses)* Especially you.

LIGHTS FADE OUT.

<u>SONG</u>

<u>SONG</u>

Scene 6

LIGHTS COME UP to reveal the HOWE LIVING ROOM. ETHAN is seated on the couch using his laptop.

LISA

There you are. I've been looking for you.

ETHAN

Hey.

LISA

What'cha doing?

ETHAN

Playing Mario.

LISA

Well..uh...hey. You wanna hear some good news?

ETHAN

Sure.

LISA

Well...remember how you asked me about the line for Jesus?

ETHAN

Yeah...you were like freaked out.

LISA

Well... I was surprised. Anyways...it sorta got me thinking. So then Julie answered a lot of questions I had and then you know what? I got it! I understood for the first time in my whole life what Christmas was all about. Y'know, that it's really about Jesus. And that He came into this world and then He gave His life for me. So... I made a decision to accept the gift of Jesus. I guess I'm a Christian now.

ETHAN

Hey, Mom. That's so cool! So you gonna come to church now?

LISA

(Happily)

You betcha.

ETHAN

What about Dad? Does he know?

LISA

Not yet.

ETHAN

Hmm. He's probably not going to be too excited.

LISA

Probably not at first. But we'll work on him. Whad'ya say?

ETHAN

Okay. Deal.

LISA

Say...wanta go to the Mall with me? I want to get a gift for someone.

ETHAN

Do I have to see Santa again?

LISA

No. You're a little too old for Santa. But maybe we can look for that line for Jesus?

ETHAN

Really? Okay. Let's go.

LISA

All right. Let's go.

<u>SONG</u>

<u>SONG</u>

<u>SONG</u>

<u>SONG</u>

MESSAGE

Scene 7

LIGHTS COME UP to reveal the MAIN STREET MALL.

ETHAN ENTERS and slowly walks by himself on the stage. As he looks up he sees two different lines with a variety of people standing in them. Above one line there is a large sign that says "TOYS FOR ORPHANS". Above the other line is another sign that says "HOLIDAY FOOD DONATIONS".

ETHAN

Hey, mom...Mom! Hurry up! You won't believe what I found.

LISA

What?

ETHAN

C'mon. You'll see.

LISA

This better be good.

ETHAN

It is. It is. Let's go.

LISA

All right, I'm coming. What did you find anyway?

ETHAN

You'll see,

LISA and ETHAN arrive on stage and she sees the lines.

LISA

Okay. What?

ETHAN

Don't you see it?

LISA

See what? Ethan...what do you see?

ETHAN

There's a line for Jesus!

LISA

What? All I see is a sign that says "Toys for Orphans"? Ooooh! I see it. You're right! There is a line. There is a line for Jesus. Do you want to get in it?

ETHAN

Sure. But don't we need to buy a present for someone first?

LISA

(Holds her hand out)

Well then let's go get one. What do you think a little boy would like for Christmas?

LISA and ETHAN begin to head off stage.

ETHAN

Well...maybe he would like a dump truck, or a stomp rocket...or maybe a Lego set....or...a..Spider man doll.

LISA

Ethan...are those things that you want for Christmas?

ETHAN

Naw Mom...I'm too old for that stuff.

LISA

Yes you are.

LISA and ETHAN continue walking.

LISA

(Tousles ETHAN'S hair)

...but maybe your father isn't....

LISA and ETHAN EXIT,

LIGHTS FADE OUT.

MESSAGE

<u>SONG</u>

The Second Chance

By Skip Martin

OVERTURE

SONG

Scene 1

LIGHTS COME UP.

It is early evening in the conference room of the offices of Morgan, Preston, and James. ROBERT PRESTON is standing next to a conference table having an energetic conversation on the telephone. Occasionally, he pauses to give instructions to his assistant, SHELLY.

ROBERT

(Animated)

Now, George. I wanna make sure you understand me. When trading opens tomorrow, we're gonna start at four two five on silver. What?...I know tomorrow's Christmas...did I say tomorrow? Well, I meant Wednesday, not tomorrow.. Hey...I'll be here tomorrow. Somebody's gotta keep the shop running.... I still don't understand why the rest of the world finds it necessary to take a day off.

ALEX walks in and hears that last part of Robert's conversation.

ALEX

(Shaking head)

I hope you're not working on Christmas...again.

ROBERT

(Putting hand over phone)

You're getting soft in your old age Alex. In this game the hustler's win, the loafers lose.

ALEX

Don't forget where you learned that from. I was doing this when you were a snot-nosed kid. And no, I'm not getting soft, I've just realized that there is more to life than just making money.

ROBERT

That's what all the wimps say. *(Back on phone*) Look...go be like all the other lemmings and take your merry day off. But be ready for that conference come 7:00 am Wednesday morning, got that? And George...keep your cell on tomorrow in case there's some developments. Right. *(Hangs up and turns to Shelly*) Remind everyone of the 7:00 meeting.

SHELLY

I already have, Mr. Preston. Is there anything else?

ROBERT

Yeah. I want everyone's cell phone number, just in case something happens tomorrow.

SHELLY

On Christmas day?

ROBERT

(Mocking) On Christmas day? I don't care if it's the Tooth Fairy's birthday. Look, we're here for one thing. It's to make money; and if we're not making it...somebody else is.

ALEX

All right Shelly. You can leave those numbers on Robert's desk. Go on home. It's six o'clock. I'm sure your family's waiting.

SHELLY

Thank you Mr. Morgan.

SHELLY exits stage right.

ROBERT

You didn't used to be so soft Alex. I remember one Christmas when we were here until midnight putting together that deal on sugar. Man, we made a killing on that one. Now, that was a Christmas celebration worth having.

ALEX

(Chuckling)

I was a younger man then. Robert...sometimes when you get a little older you get a little more wisdom. You know, there's more to life than money.

SHELLY enters stage right.

SHELLY

Sorry to interrupt you...but there's a phone message here from a Ms. English.

ROBERT

Put it over there.

SHELLY walks over and places it on the desk.

ALEX

Merry Christmas

SHELLY

Good night. Merry Christmas.

ROBERT

(Waving her off)

Yeah, yeah...Merry Christmas.

SHELLY exits stage right.

ROBERT

If there's something better than money, I'm not interested in it. Alex...this is what I love. All of this. I mean I love the work, I love the feeling you get when the heart starts pumping. I love the sweat on the palms. And I love closing the deal. Most of all...I love the money. Man, I just love the way it feels, I love the way it smells...all of it.

ALEX

Yeah...that'll make a great epitaph. "Robert Preston. He loved the smell of money." Robert what kind of legacy are you going to have?

ROBERT

Legacy? That's hokum. What does that have to do with anything?

ALEX

(Shakes head)

It's a whale of lot more important than what you do here.

ROBERT

(Snorts)

Whatever.

ALEX

Well, son...one day I hope you'll wake up and smell the coffee. You only get so many chances. *(Gets up to leave*) Hey...everyone else is gone. I've gotta go. Don't stay too late. And...uh...Merry Christmas.

ROBERT

(Sarcastically)

Right, Merry Christmas.

As ALEX exits stage right, ROBERT walks over to his desk and picks up a stack of messages and starts going through them. Suddenly, he stops and looks at one of them.

ROBERT

Julie English? I haven't seen her in ten years. Wonder how she's doing?

After a few moments he stuffs the message slip into his pocket, picks up his coat and exits stage right.

LIGHTS FADE OUT.

<u>SONG</u>

Scene 2

LIGHTS COME UP.

The lights come up as ROBERT enters stage left. As he fumbles with the keys to his apartment, he doesn't notice a STRANGER dressed in a white tuxedo who is standing nearby, leaning on a cane. There is also a package by the side of the door.

STRANGER

Don't forget the package.

ROBERT

Oh...yeah. Thanks.

ROBERT eyes the stranger suspiciously, then bends to pick it up.

STRANGER

(Rushes to help with package)

Where are my manners? Please... allow me.

They have brief tug-of-war over the package before ROBERT prevails. He is now a bit perturbed as the stranger is now blocking his entry to the door.

ROBERT

Do you mind?

STRANGER

Oh...no. Not at all. By all means.

ROBERT

All right...all right...look...need some money? Here's twenty dollars. I'm sure that'll buy you all the booze you want. Now, if you don't mind I have plans for this evening.

STRANGER

Like what?

ROBERT finally gets door open and steps inside with package as the stranger follows.

ROBERT

That is none of your beeswax.

STRANGER

Ah...contrare. It's very much my business. In fact, that's why I'm here. *(Pulls out a card and looks at it)* Let's see...Robert Preston. You're not married, have no children, no cats and no dogs. You do have a Maserati, a rather nice portfolio with Smith Barney and.....a very nice place on the Jersey shore...ah... and I almost forgot...a condo on Longboat Key. But you're not very happy with your life are you?

ROBERT

Oh...I get it. Alex put you up to this. Oh no...he's not going to pull that on me. *(Steps out the door)* Alex, Alex! Wherever you are...come on out. Alex?

STRANGER

Alex has nothing to do with this, Robert. I'm here because you're not happy.

ROBERT

What do you mean I'm not happy? *(Puts down package)* Of course, I'm happy. I've got everything I want. Wait a minute...why am I even talking to you?

STRANGER

Beats me. There's certainly no law that says you have to.

ROBERT

Who are you anyway? How do you know that stuff about me? I think I'm going to call the police.

STRANGER

Suit yourself. Phone's over there. I believe the number is 9-1-1. (*Walks over and picks up package)* By the way...I wouldn't mention the part about the package, you know...that you got from Julie English....the way tensions are these days they'll probably send the bomb squad.

ROBERT

(Holding phone in hand)

Julie English sent that? *(Hangs up phone and walks over to where the STRANGER is standing)* Give me that!

STRANGER

Robert? Don't you remember? It was ten years ago today that you made a decision that changed your life.

ROBERT

What are you talking about?

STRANGER

It was ten years ago. You and Julie. She made a decision to become a follower of Christ, and you were going to join her. But well...you know the rest of the story...

ROBERT

Has it been ten years?

STRANGER

Ten years to the day.

ROBERT

I had no idea.

STRANGER

You were ready to make that decision, weren't you? You just wanted to do one more thing. I think what you told Julie was...that you were going to go home first, sell your house, and work for a few months so that you could get the finances in order. Then you were going to join her. But, life has a funny way of working out doesn't it Robert? Look where you are now.

ROBERT

Hey, I've got a plan. Once I've made enough money, I'll be free do what I want. There's plenty of time. I'm still in the prime of life.

ROBERT moves over to the bar and begins mixing himself a drink.

STRANGER

Sometimes you never get another chance, Robert. One day you're crossing the street, and the next minute a car comes around the corner...and *(Snaps fingers)* that's it. Look back at September 11.

ROBERT

So...you know Julie? How's she doing?

STRANGER

Julie? She's living a life of full of little blessings everyday. You could be too.

ROBERT

What are you talking about? Look around you. I've got everything I need. There isn't anything I don't have.

STRANGER

(Moves to door)

"There isn't anything I don't have." Okay. Those were your words. Think about it Robert. Remember, life doesn't always give a second chance.

STRANGER exits stage left.

ROBERT

I don't need to think about it. And please don't bother me again or I will call the police. So, please spare me the trouble.

ROBERT loosens his tie, and after taking a large gulp of his drink lies down, deep in thought.

ROBERT

He's right about one thing. I need better security around here.

LIGHTS FADE OUT.

SONG

SONG

Scene 3

LIGHTS COME UP.

It is morning on Christmas day. As ROBERT slowly wakens and stretches. JULIE is seated at her vanity putting on makeup.

ROBERT

Oh, thank God. What a nightmare. What was with that guy in the white tuxedo?

JULIE

What guy?

ROBERT

What on earth?

JULIE

(Mumbling)

Whad' you say?

ROBERT

Um...excuse me...I don't mean to be rude. But...can I ask what you're doing here?

JULIE

Umph? What am I doing here?

ROBERT

Yes. What are you doing here?

JULIE

The same thing I've been doing every other morning of our marriage. Oh..my goodness. Look at the time. I've got to wrap those last presents. Robby, I need your help. Would you...

ROBERT

Julie?

JULIE

(Yawning)

What, Robert?

ROBERT

Julie...I can't believe its you.

JULIE

(Defensively touches face)

What did you expect....Julia Roberts?

ROBERT

No...no. I just can't believe its you.

JULIE

(Staring cooly)

Robert. I have got ten gazillion things to do this morning. Okay so cut it out.

JULIE rushes to put her things together.

JULIE

I'm supposed to be at the Children's Home at 9:00 to give out presents.

ROBERT

What children's home?

JULIE

What children's home? Robert is something wrong with you? Because you're acting really strange. You know we always go to Bayshore Children's Home on Christmas Day.

ROBERT

Well to be perfectly honest with you, I feel like I'm in the Twilight Zone right now. But I'm fine...there's nothing wrong with me...its just that everything looks so...realistic.

JULIE

Robert. I appreciate your sense of humor. In fact its one of the things I love about you. But right now...I just want you to cut it out.

JULIE exits stage left.

ROBERT

Okay. Guess I'll just play this by ear.

LIGHTS FADE OUT.

<u>SONG</u>

Scene 4

LIGHTS COME UP.

JULIE and MRS. JONES enter from stage left.

MRS. JONES

Thank you so much for coming Julie. The children look forward so much to your visits. It is especially hard for them on Christmas.

JULIE

Please Mrs. Jones. Really, the pleasure is mine. I enjoy so much seeing their eyes light up.

MRS. JONES

Oh, dear...have we lost Mr. Preston?

JULIE

What? Oh..Robert, are you coming?

FROM OFFSTAGE.

ROBERT

I'm coming...I'm coming.

ROBERT enters from stage left, he is so overloaded with gifts and presents, that it appears that he may spill them at any moment.

ROBERT

(With strain in his voice)

Can I help it if Rudolph decides to take the day off? How many kids do you have in this place anyway?

MRS. JONES

Oh, dear. We have twenty five beds. And we're usually always full. Of course, today, many of them are out on home visits. Um...perhaps you should put those down over there. *(Points to Christmas tree)*

ROBERT shuffles over to the tree and MRS. JONES and JULIE help him put down the presents.

ROBERT

Nice tree.

MRS. JONES

Yes, lovely, isn't it. We have one donated every year by the members of First Baptist Church. You know, the one down on Main Street.

ROBERT

Yes. I've heard of that one. Well...where are the children?

MRS. JONES

Well...if you're ready, I'll call them right now.

MRS. JONES walks over to a stand where there is a bell, and picking it up, rings it.

FIVE CHILDREN, full of excitement, come noisily running in from stage right. They are of various ages, dressed with clothes which are obviously hand- me- down.

MRS JONES

(Clapping hands)

Children...children. Line up.

The FIVE CHILDREN line up with military precision at MRS. JONES command.

MRS. JONES

Children...I believe some of you have met Mrs. Preston before. And this is Mr. Preston. We are thankful that they have come to visit us today. I think they may have brought a little something with them.

JULIE

Good morning, children.

CHILDREN

Good morning, Mrs. Preston.

JULIE

I'm so happy to see all of you today. Does anybody know the story of Baby Jesus and the Wise Men?

FIRST GIRL

I do..I do.

JULIE

What did the Wise Men come to do?

OLDER GIRL

They came to give presents.

JULIE

That's exactly right. It says in the Bible that they brought gifts of Gold, Frankincense and Myrrh after that very first Christmas. So we follow that example when we give gifts in celebration of Jesus' birthday today.

FIRST BOY

That's my favorite part.

JULIE

Mine too. But did you know that there was an important gift even before the Wise Men?

CHILDREN

No.

JULIE

The very first Christmas gift was Jesus. He was God's gift to us. Because we are so thankful for God's gift, we honor Him by giving gifts to others. We hope you will enjoy these gifts and that they will help you remember that God loves you.

SECOND BOY

Can we open them now...Mrs. Jones?

OTHER KIDS

Can we? Can we?

MRS. JONES

Yes, you may.

THE CHILDREN all run over to the pile of gifts and begin to shred them open. In their eagerness to unwrap them, they fail to notice that a small child is left out and too shy to join the crowd. As the others shriek with joy, she begins to well up with tears. Finally, the oldest child notices her and leaves the crowd to bring her a large gift. Opening it, she pulls out a large stuffed teddy bear.

OLDER GIRL

Here, Amy. Why don't you have this one?

THE YOUNG CHILD stops sniffling and smiles as she accepts the teddy bear and hugs the older child.

MRS. JONES

I think the spirit of Christmas is here at last.

LIGHTS FADE OUT.

<u>SONG</u>

SONG

Scene 5

LIGHTS COME UP on the upper stage.

ROBERT and STRANGER are on the upper stage. STRANGER is dressed in a brown uniform, similar to a UPS delivery man, and has just delivered a package to ROBERT.

STRANGER

New computer monitor, huh?

ROBERT

Yeah. Need to upgrade the system. Trying to follow the...markets.

STRANGER

Oh, yeah. You one of those on-line traders?

ROBERT

Nah. That's child's play. I like commodities. You know oil, gold, silver, pork bellies...

STRANGER

Oh, yeah. I was just reading about this guy who was trying to corner the market on silver. Imagine that. I mean how would you even spend all that money?

ROBERT

I could think of a lot of ways. You look familiar. Don't I know you from somewhere?

STRANGER

Oh...I've been around. Sign here please.

ROBERT signs the sheet.

ROBERT

I could swear I've seen you before.

STRANGER

Well, I don't know anything about commodity markets, but I do know a little bit about things that have a more lasting value.

ROBERT

More lasting value? What's more lasting than gold or silver?

STRANGER

Things that last forever.

ROBERT

What do you mean?

STRANGER

Come... watch...I'll think I'll let Julie show you that.

LIGHTS COME UP on center stage. They dim somewhat on the upper stage.

JULIE knocks on the door of a modest home. After several loud knocks a small girl shyly answers the door.

JULIE

Hello. Is your mother home?

GIRL

She's in there.

Her MOTHER calls from offstage.

MOTHER

Who is it?

JULIE

I'm Julie Preston. Mrs. Jones from Children's Home asked me to come by.

MOTHER

Oh. I wasn't expectin' nobody.

JULIE

I'm sorry. If this is a bad time, I can...I can come back?

MOTHER

No. Never mind. Come on it. I'm so sick, I don't know how much longer I'll be.

JULIE

Yes. I'm sorry.

MOTHER

(Coughing and hacking)

Have a seat over there. This here is Paula.

JULIE

I'm so glad to meet you. You're such a pretty little girl.

MOTHER

Don't understand it a'tall. She's special that one. I'm not afraid of dying, but I'm sceared of what's gonna happen to her.

JULIE

What about her father?

MOTHER

Ah can't count on him none. If and when he gets out of prison, I'm sure he'll go back to drinkin' just like he always does.

JULIE

There's hope for everyone. Mrs. Johnson.

MOTHER

(Shakes head between coughs)

I've lived a hard life. One thing I've learned is be realistic. Do you believe in Angels?

JULIE

The Bible speaks of them. So I know that they are true.

MOTHER

That Paula...sometimes I think she's one. She's what's keepin' me alive. But now I'm at the point where I'm not sure even that's workin'. Doctor says the cancer's all over me now. I won't be able to stay home much longer.

JULIE

Mrs. Johnson, when Paula gets placed with Children's Home, I'd like to take her to church. I've come to ask your permission. In fact, I'd love to take her before then...this Sunday.

MOTHER

Mrs. Jones with Children's Home. She came highly recommended. So I guess you're okay.

JULIE

She's one of God's pecious ones, Mrs. Johnson. I'll guard her with my life. Can I get you anything at the store?

LIGHTS FADE OUT on the upper stage and STRANGER and ROBERT exit.

MOTHER

Thank you kindly. I don't recken I need anything right now. I 'preciate you askin. And...I thank you for takin Paula to church. I always wanted her to get some church learnin.

JULIE

This is what I'm called to do. Mrs. Johnson, she'll be in good hands with Children's Home. I promise you. I'll come by about 9:00 o'clock. Okay. *(Bends down to talk to Paula)* I look forward to seeing you on Sunday. Bye now.

LIGHTS FADE OUT.

<u>SONG</u>

<u>SONG</u>

Scene 6

LIGHTS COME UP as we see JULIE praying on knees.

JULIE

Lord, I've felt your presence today. Thank you for blessing us with your presence.

ROBERT enters from stage left. He appears concerned and is holding a bill in his hand. Just as he is about to speak, he stops as he notices that JULIE is praying.

JULIE

Open my eyes so that I may see where you are working and that I may join you in your work. I pray this in Jesus name. Amen.

ROBERT

Ahem...speaking of working...did you know that we haven't paid the electric bill this month?

JULIE

Oh...I didn't realize that.

ROBERT

Did you realize that we have exactly eleven dollars and thirty seven cents in the bank?

JULIE

Really? We have that much? Maybe we should give it Children's Home?

ROBERT

Very funny. You know. That's it. That's all we have. Eleven dollars and thirty seven cents.

JULIE

Yes, Robert. I heard you the first time. Are you worried?

ROBERT

No. I'm not worried. Its just that the rent is due. The water bill hasn't been paid. The electric bill hasn't been paid. Aren't you just a little bit worried?

JULIE

Robert. Dear Robert. It says in the scriptures: "Do not worry, saying, what shall we eat or what shall we drink or what shall we wear? Jesus said seek first His kingdom and His righteousness, and these things shall be given to you as well."

ROBERT

Well that's all very fine for you to say, but I'm not used to this. We owe five hundred and thirty for the rent, sixty five for the electric, and thirty for the water. That's six hundred and twenty five in case you didn't do the math. Look Julie, maybe we should have a talk. Maybe instead of this ministry thing...I could get a regular job. Then we wouldn't have to worry about money. I could do something like work for a brokerage firm. I think I might have a talent for uh..trading things.

JULIE

(Reproachfully)

A brokerage firm? Robert.

ROBERT

What? All right. I'll have...faith. Look, maybe you could just add a little... request the next time you pray...you know..for a little extra cash.

JULIE

Ye of little faith. All it takes is a mustard seed's worth you know. And no, I'm not going to pray for "a little extra cash". He knows what we need, and I'm sure that He will provide. Did you get the mail?

ROBERT

Yeah. But I didn't have the heart to look at it. I don't want to deal with any more bills. It's there...over there on the kitchen table.

JULIE walks over and picks up the stack of mail. As she glances through, one catches her eye.

JULIE

There's a letter from South Dakota. Do you know anyone there?

ROBERT

South Dakota? Better make sure there's no powder in it.

JULIE glares at ROBERT then tears open the letter and begins to read it.

JULIE

Dear Mrs. Preston. I've been looking for a ministry to support. God has placed upon my heart the desire to help someone who is working with children. I pray that this modest check will help you to continue your wonderful work. Yours in Christ. A Christian in Sioux Falls. Look...here's a check. Robert, how much did you say those bills were?

ROBERT

Oh...uh..six hundred and twenty five. Why?

JULIE

This is a check for six hundred and twenty five dollars.

LIGHTS FADE OUT.

<u>SONG</u>

Scene 7

LIGHTS COME UP as JULIE is working at her desk. She has a Bible spread open and is making notes on a legal pad. ROBERT enters carrying a copy of the Wall Street Journal.

ROBERT

What 'ya doin?

JULIE

Preparing the Sunday School lesson. How 'bout you?

ROBERT

Oh...just looking at the...you know...the Journal.

JULIE

The Journal? As in the Wall Street Journal?

ROBERT

(Sheepishly nods for a few moments)

Yeah.

JULIE

Do you think that you might be just a little preoccupied with money?

ROBERT

Well...I wouldn't say that...

JULIE

Robert. "Do not store up for yourselves treasure on earth where moth and rust destroy, and where thieves break in and steal". "But store up for yourselves treasures in heaven where moth and rust do not destroy"

ROBERT

Okay. I can't quote the scriptures like that. So I'm not going to get into that battle. But can I just....can I ask you something?

JULIE

It'll cost you.

ROBERT

Seriously.

JULIE

Okay. Go ahead.

ROBERT

How can you be so sure in your faith?

JULIE

Do you want the short version or the long version?

ROBERT

I think I'm ready for the long.

JULIE

Okay. Well...I guess it started when there was point in my life where I asked God what does all this mean? Why am I here? What about the Bible? How do I know its true? I wanted an answer to those questions, so I began a spiritual journey. And along the way I met someone who had experienced God in her life. I mean really experienced God. And through that person I began to realize that God is not just some figure in the Bible...or some ancient being or faraway presence. That...that He's really with me now, and I can live in His presence and can experience Him every day. After I realized that...I believed. Since then, the more I read His word, the more I experience Him in my life, and the more I experience Him, the stronger my faith becomes.

ROBERT

You make it sound so simple.

JULIE

In a way it is. Robby can I ask you something?

ROBERT

Yeah, sure. What?

JULIE

Is there something you're not telling me? You've been acting a little strange lately. Talking about working for a brokerage firm, reading the Wall Street Journal...I don't understand?

ROBERT

Julie...I don't even know how to begin. I've been trying to think of a way to explain it...but I can't...not yet. I'm sorry... I just can't talk about it right now.

ROBERT hurriedly exits stage left.

LIGHTS FADE OUT.

<u>SONG</u>

<u>SONG</u>

Scene 8

LIGHTS COME UP as ROBERT is sleeping. JULIE is watching him from the vanity. She noisily places a package by the side of the bed, as she unobtrusively tries to wake up ROBERT, until finally, he starts to awaken.

ROBERT

Oh, uh....mornin.

JULIE

I don't see how you do it.

ROBERT

Do what?

JULIE

How you could sleep so late today?

ROBERT

(Yawning)

It's only seven-thirty. What's so special about today?

JULIE

Oh...you're not playing that game with me. You know what today is.

ROBERT

You mean...it's our....it's our wedding anniversary? Honey...I can't believe that I forgot. I don't know what to say.

JULIE

Robert, you know it's not our wedding anniversary.

ROBERT

It's not?

JULIE

No. You're not going to get me this time. *(Reaching for gift)* Here...this is for you.

ROBERT

(Opening present)

It's a book. "Angels. God's Secret Agents" by Billy Graham.

JULIE

This was so you. I mean...you kinda of have that thing about Angels.

ROBERT

Great. This is uh...great. You always pick the perfect gift. Thank you.

JULIE

Well..Okay. I'll make it easy for you. I'll close my eyes.

ROBERT

Julie...I uh...forgot what today is. I don't know. I must be..you know...going senile or something.

JULIE

(Opening eyes)

Are you serious? You don't remember. Ten years ago...today. You accepted Christ. You became a Christian....a follower. I can't believe it. How could you forget the most important day of your life?

ROBERT

I don't know what to say.

JULIE

Robert, I don't know what's gotten into you. But it's starting to get me worried. Whatever it is I hope you'll take it to the Lord in prayer. Lord knows, I've been praying for you all I can.

JULIE exits stage right.

ROBERT

Why does everybody keep reminding me of this day, ten years ago? You'd think eternity rested on it or something.

STRANGER steps from around the TREE.

STRANGER

As a matter of fact it does.

ROBERT

You! It's you! You're the one who did this to me.

STRANGER

No, Robert you did this to yourself. Remember, your own words. "There's isn't anything I don't have." Still feel the same way?

ROBERT

I know I said that. But it was just an off-hand remark...I really didn't mean it.

STRANGER

You've had an opportunity to see what could have been. To look down the path not taken. But when you wake up. You'll be back where you were. Everything after that is up to you.

ROBERT

No. Don't do that. I want to stay here.

STRANGER

It doesn't work that way. *(Takes book from Robert)* Good book. Look, I don't set the rules. I just follow orders. Just, remember, you never know if you'll get a second chance.

ROBERT

Wait. Don't go. I've made a decision. I don't want to lose Julie.

LIGHTS FADE OUT.

<u>SONG</u>

Scene 9

LIGHTS COME UP.

It is the morning after Christmas. Robert slowly stretches as he starts to awaken. The PHONE rings loudly, jarring him to his senses.

ROBERT

Hello. Shelly? It's seven o'clock? Everyone's waiting for me? Look, Shelly, hold on a second. *(Looking around)* Julie? Julie? She's gone. Everything's gone. *(Goes back on phone)* Shelly, is Alex there? Good put him on. *(Pauses)* Alex. I've had an extraordinary experience. No, no. Nothing like that. I need some time to take care of a few things. Can you take over the silver deal? I don't care how you do it...you can cancel the whole thing if you want... I know I put a lot of time into it...but you know what...right now...it just doesn't matter. Thanks, Alex. I'll give you a call later.

ROBERT hangs up the phone and begins looking around until he finds the package. He opens it and begins to smile widely when he realizes what is inside.

ROBERT

My angels. She sent my angels. I can't believe she kept them all these years.

ROBERT realizes with a start that he also has a phone message from JULIE.

ROBERT

Where did I put that number?

ROBERT looks around for a few moments without success in finding the number until at last he thinks to look in his jacket, where he finally finds the missing phone message. He quickly strides to the phone and dials the number.

ROBERT

Hello. Um...May I speak to Julie...Julie English? She's not? She's going where? When will she be back? Look...can you take a message...its from an old friend. Robert, Robert Preston. I need to talk to her before she goes. It's very important. Tell her I got the angels and I really appreciate her thinking to send them, and... and...tell her I've just made the most important decision of my life...and to not leave until I get a chance to talk to her. Yeah. Oh...what's the address. Hold on. I need to write that down *(Looks around for and finds a scrap of paper and pen)* Okay. Go ahead. 58 Roman Road. Got it. Thanks, Thanks a lot.

LIGHTS FADE OUT.

<u>SONG</u>

<u>SONG</u>

Scene 10

LIGHTS COME UP.

ROBERT is out of breath as he enters. Checking the address, he straightens himself and knocks on the door.

JULIE

Robert, I can't believe its you. When I got your message I assumed it must be a mistake. You know...since you're so rich and famous. How many years has it been?

ROBERT

Ten. It's been ten years. I uh...I got your package.

JULIE

Oh...good. I'm glad.

ROBERT

Listen. Can we talk?

JULIE

Of course...but I'm afraid I don't have long. *(She motions toward several suitcases positioned near the door)*

ROBERT

Yes, I heard. You're going to the Dominican Republic?

JULIE

Yes. There's an orphanage in Santo Domingo that really needs someone.. There's so much of God's work to do, and I'm very excited.

ROBERT

Do you believe in second chances?

JULIE

Well...sure...as a Christian I believe that Jesus gives us second chances every day.

ROBERT

No. I mean for us.

JULIE

Oh...that was a long time ago, Robert.

ROBERT

Yes. I know.. But I wasn't a Christian then. And now...I am.

JULIE

Robert Preston, I've prayed for you each and every day for the last ten years, and I've never given up hope that you would accept Christ into your heart. But when did it happen?

ROBERT

This morning. It won't make any sense...but here goes. Last night I had this wonderful and amazing dream. I dreamed about this really strange person...I guess he was an angel...and you were in it. And because of the dream, basically, I realized I've been running for the last ten years. I don't know what I was so afraid of? I guess I was afraid of all things that I would have to give up if I was to follow God's way. But this dream was a strange and wonderful opportunity to see what my life could have been like if I had just been willing to follow God's plan.. It was wonderful. I realized that He really does care about me and He wants the best for me. And if I just trust Him, I'm not really losing anything, and I'm gaining everything.

JULIE

Robert, that's wonderful. I can hardly believe its true. I just wish it could have happened ten years ago.

ROBERT

Julie. God's given me a second chance. And I'm asking...can you give me a second chance too? I miss you, Julie. I miss you teasing me with your quotes of Scriptures. I miss your quiet strength. I miss the look on your face when you're talking to the children. I even miss those silly Snoopy slippers.

JULIE

Robert...how did you know I have Snoopy slippers?

ROBERT

If I told you, you'd never believe me.

JULIE

(Glancing at watch) Tell you what. Looks like we have some catching up to do. Why don't we go to Starbucks and get some coffee?

ROBERT

What about your flight?

JULIE

Something tells me that it can wait. I've waited ten years for this. And I really don't plan on having to wait another ten.

LIGHTS FADE OUT.

MESSAGE

<u>SONG</u>

The Innkeeper's Vision

By Skip Martin

OVERTURE

Scene 1

LIGHTS COME UP.

It is mid-morning at the Osprey Bed and Breakfast. It is Christmas time and the lobby is festively decorated for the season. An elderly gentleman strides briskly in and approaches the front desk. Seeing no one, he impatiently rings the bell on the desk. After several rings, each increasing in loudness, DANIEL SHEPARD, the innkeeper hurries in from stage left.

DAN

Okay, okay. I'm coming...I'm coming. Yes..Mr. Dangler. What can possibly be so important that you can't wait ten seconds?

DANGLER

Young man. I am a paying customer... and the customer is always right.

DAN

(Biting his tongue with difficulty)

Of course. Whatever you say. Just understand one thing. I haven't had much sleep. Okay. All right. So...please...Mr. Dangler could you just tell me what you want?

DANGLER

Young man, I didn't get my paper this morning. I always get the paper in the morning and this morning I didn't get my paper. So I had to put on my loafers and go out on my own to get a paper. So what have you to say about that young man?

DAN

Look, Mr....uh...Mr...uh...

DANGLER

Dangler.

DAN

Thank you. Look, my night clerk quit yesterday so last night I was the night clerk. I haven't been able to hire a housekeeper in two weeks...

DANGLER

No excuses, young man. No excuses!You need to have a little better service around here, or I may have to take my business someplace else. *(Leaving)* We have much better service than this up north.

DANGLER EXITS. Almost immediately, SARAH enters carrying a ledger and a pencil in her mouth.

DAN

Why do I even try?

SARAH

Umph.

DAN

What?

SARAH

Umph. Umph.

DAN

Am I supposed to understand that?

SARAH

(Exasperated)

I was just saying, why do you even try?

DAN

I don't know. I thought perhaps you would have the answer. You always do. I certainly don't.

SARAH

Well, don't get cross with me just because you're having a bad day.

DAN

No, I'm not having a bad day. I'm having a bad life. You know, you can't find any help now if your life depended on it. And do you want to know how much they want now? Do you want to know? That last...punk...I interviewed said he wanted fifteen an hour to start. Fifteen dollars! To be a desk clerk! Not to mention a 401(k) plan, three weeks paid vacation, five personal days...oh...and a thousand dollar sign up bonus.

SARAH

Look, you're the one who decided that you wanted to own a bed and breakfast. It wasn't me. And you're the one who wanted to sell Beanie Babies on the internet. Yeah, that turned out to be a great idea. Let's see, before that there was that little video store...oh that one was REALLY good. One week after it opened...Blockbuster moved next door. So...okay, this bed and breakfast is a lot of work, and we don't get any vacation time, and we can't afford health insurance and we're not making any money...but you know what...I am not leaving.

SARAH storms out stage left.

DAN

What did I say? Oh, well. Guess now's not a good time to talk to her about that scooter store idea.

LIGHTS FADE OUT.

<u>SONG</u>

Scene 2

LIGHTS COME UP.

DAN ENTERS from stage right.

DAN

Ruth, can you hurry it up a little bit with those eggs. If Mr. Dangler eats any more bagels he's going to think he's at a bar mitzvah.

SARAH ENTERS walking quickly. She is carrying a juice pitcher.

SARAH

The way these people drink orange juice you'd think this was their last breakfast.

DAN

The way Ruth cooks, it might be.

SARAH

(Grimacing)

Dan, don't start with Ruth. You know how hard it is to find a good cook.

DAN

The cook part I'll give you. Good? I don't think I'd go that far.

SARAH glares at DAN.

DAN

All right...all right. But I'll bet you there's not another bed and breakfast in Florida that can say that they had their Thanksgiving turkey stuffed with sauerkraut.

RUTH ENTERS from stage left.

RUTH

Did I hear you guys talking about me?

SARAH AND DAN

No.

RUTH

I could have sworn I heard my name.

DAN

Oh...that. I was just telling Sarah of how...creative you could be.

RUTH

Oh.

DAN

Did you bring the eggs?

RUTH

(With sarcasm)

What do these look like?

DAN

Are those...scrambled?

RUTH

Of course. Whad'ya think they were...fried?

DAN

Um...just wanted to make sure. Here, I'll take those. *(To Sarah).* We'll try Mr. Dangler. He doesn't see to well.

DANIEL EXITS stage left.

RUTH

(Puzzled)

What did he mean by that?

SARAH

Oh..nothing. You know him. Always joking. Perhaps you should try some waffles? We haven't had those in awhile.

RUTH

Waffles are so... ordinary. But...maybe if I put some cherries in it and add a little coconut...

RUTH EXITS deep in thought. SARAH can't help smiling as she picks up the mail and begins sorting through it. SAM ENTERS.

SAM

Hey, Sarah. What's cookin?

SARAH

Oh...Hi, Sam. Nothing much. You know how things are around here.

SAM

Is..uh...Danny boy up yet.

SARAH

Yes. He's serving breakfast. He'll be back in a second. How's the golf game coming?

SAM

Not bad. I only lost five balls yesterday.

SARAH

Hm...that's good. Why don't you make yourself at home? I'm sure Dan will be glad to see you.

SARAH EXITS. SAM walks around the counter and picks up a magazine that catches his eye.

DANIEL comes back in carrying the serving tray.

SAM

Hey, Dan. What's up?

DAN

Whazzup.

SAM

(Swings imaginary golf club)

Wanna play?

DAN

Nah, Sam, I can't. I've just got too much I've got to do here.

SAM

That's what you said last time...and the time before that. Something wrong?

DAN

What? Nah. I'm allright.

SAM

Dan, I've been you're friend for a long time. You can't pull the wool over my eyes. Something's bugging you isn't it?

DAN

No. Really there isn't.

SAM

Hey buddy, you forget. I've known you for over twenty years. I was your best man. I'm your golfing buddy. I *know* when something's bugging you.

DAN

Okay. All right. You're right. Something is bugging me.

SAM

All right, what gives? What is it?

DAN

Oh, I don't know. I just...I just can't seem to get into the Christmas spirit. I mean every year we go through all this trouble, with the decorations and all and then with presents, and all we do is get deeper into debt. I'm not even sure what it all means anymore.

SAM

Hey...I've got the perfect cure. Eighteen holes of golf.

DAN

I don't think so.

SAM

Hey, I was just kiddin'. Look, I've been there before. But now Christmas means a whole lot more to me. You know...since...

DAN

Yeah. I know. You had some sort of spiritual experience.

SAM

It was more than just an experience Dan. It's a whole new understanding of what life means. Have you ever given any thought to what that first Christmas really meant?

DAN

That first Christmas?

SAM

Yeah.

DAN

You mean the *first* Christmas. The one with the manger, and the wise men and all that?

SAM nods.

DAN

Well you know Sam, that's just for kids and stuff.

SAM

Oh, really?

DAN

All right now, don't give me that look.

SAM

Moi?

DAN

Look, I'm sure that.....Jesus...was born and all that. And...and....maybe those, uh...stargazers really thought they were following a moving star, but the virgin birth? I don't think so. And those angels, probably not. I guess you might say I just don't believe in miracles.

SAM

Dan, take a deep breath.

DAN

What?

SAM

Seriously. Take a deep breath.

Sheepishly DAN takes a deep breath then exhales.

SAM

Now, that was just a miracle.

DAN

Come on.

SAM

Think about it. That breath started with an impulse in your brain. Then your chest muscles contracted forcing your lungs to expand. Air consisting of oxygen and nitrogen rushed in filling the vacuum. The oxygen then filtered from your lungs to your blood vessels. Meanwhile your heart, controlled by electrical impulse, pumps the blood....

DAN

Okay, okay. I see your point. Look Sam, I appreciate your concern about me and all, but now's not a good time to talk about all this. I've got work to do. I'm trying to make a living. Look, let's talk about this some other time.

DAN EXITS.

SAM

Lord, I sure hope you are still in the business of working miracles, because it looks like we're gonna need one here.

LIGHTS FADE OUT.

<u>SONG</u>

Scene 3

LIGHTS COME UP.

The handyman, IKE, ENTERS. He has a carpenter's apron wrapped around his waist and is carrying a ladder.

IKE

Mr. Shepherd....Mr. Shepherd. I bought that new carpet you wanted. *(Looks around)* Mr. Shepherd? Oh, well.

SAM notices a poster on the wall which has fallen down. He picks it up and tries to hang it by the nail, however, the nail will not hold it. After several attempts, he looks both ways and then takes a wad of gum out of his mouth and sticks it onto the back of the poster. This time the picture stays in place. SAM walks behind the counter and visually explores the contents. Noticing a magazine, he picks it up for a moment before tossing it aside. Next IKE opens the guest book and taking a pen, pretends that he is DAN SHEPHARD.

IKE

(Rings desk bell)

May I help you? *(Strikes a different position)* Ahem...may I help you? *(Trying yet another position)* Yes...may I help you?

DAN ENTERS from downstage right interrupting IKE'S reverie.

DAN

May I ask what you're doing?

IKE

(So startled he throws pen in air)

Whoa...Mr. Shephard! You kinda surprised me.

DAN

I can see that. Well...I'll tell you how you can really help. Try fixing that light bulb.

DAN points to ceiling.

IKE

Mr. Shephard...uh...you won't tell anyone what I was doin' will ya? I was just tryin' to pretend I was someone important. That's all.

DAN

I guess that depends on how quickly you can change that bulb.

IKE

(Springing into action)

Uh...yes sir.

While IKE picks up the ladder and begins maneuvering it into position, DAN watches curiously.

DAN

Isn't that a little bit short?

IKE stops and looks back and forth from the ladder to the ceiling.

IKE

Uh...I guess you're right. I'll uh...I'll take this one back and get the long one.

DAN

(Pointing to corner)

Good idea. Is that the new carpet?

IKE

Yeah...yeah. Check it out while I'm gone.

IKE picks up the ladder and struggles a little to get control. To regain control, he changes his grip, and then rapidly swings it around in order to get the ladder through the door. He doesn't notice DAN who is bent over looking at the carpet. At the last instant he realizes that DAN is in the way.

IKE

Watch out!

DAN stands up just in time to be pancaked by the ladder. DAN groans as he slumps to the floor.

IKE

Mr. Shepherd? Mr. Shepherd? Are you alright? Mr. Shepherd...talk to me...talk to me Mr. Shepherd.

LIGHTS FADE DOWN.

SONG

SONG

Scene 4

LIGHTS COME UP.

DANIEL slowly awakens. He looks around, puzzled, because things are very different. There is no counter and there are no Christmas decorations. As he looks down he realizes that he is dressed in a long flowing robe of the kind used in Israel at the time of Christ. He is sitting up rubbing his head when SARAH ENTERS.

SARAH

How is it that you can sleep at such a busy time? The census is tomorrow. Even now people are arriving.

DANIEL

Where am I? Why am I dressed like this? Why are you dressed like that?

SARAH

Daniel, son of Jacob. I have no time for such foolish questions. Could you help me?

DANIEL

Sarah...what is the meaning of this? I know we need the business, but aren't these costumes going a little bit too far?

SARAH

Honestly. Sometimes I wonder about you. You have not been yourself lately. When the census is over, perhaps we should have a visit with Rabbi Eli?

DANIEL

Census...we just did a census...what census?

SARAH

Caesar's census. The one we have been preparing for all these days. Please I beg of you, I do not believe I can bear any of your joking today. There is too much work to do.

SARAH rushes out stage right.

DANIEL

Caesar's census? *(Puts hand to his head*) Ouch!

BENJAMIN ENTERS.

BENJAMIN

Peace be with you. I am Benjamin from Hebron. Have you any rooms? I'm afraid that if I have to walk another step that I shall drop. I passed no less than four caravans this day.

DANIEL

Is that so? Well..uh...sure....I mean we always have room.

BENJAMIN

If it is possible...I would like a room with a lampstand. Also I hope you have one of those beds with slats...not ropes. Better for the back you know.

DANIEL

Well the beds we have are all quite comfortable. Now about that lampstand... you know we aim to please....but I really don't want to have any trouble with the fire marshall if that's all right.

BENJAMIN

If it is too much trouble...I will take what you have. All the rooms closer to the road have been taken.

DANIEL

Fine. Just sign this....scroll?

ISAAC ENTERS. He bears a very strong resemblance to IKE.

ISAAC

Greetings, my friend. I am told that you may have rooms here?

DANIEL

Don't I know you from somewhere?

ISAAC

Have you been to Joppa?

DANIEL

No. Can't say that I have.

ISAAC

I am Isaac, a carpenter. In my village I am well known. For anything that needs fixing, they come to Isaac. Perhaps you have seen me at the market in Jerusalem?

DANIEL

Well, I've never been to Jerusalem. Who knows. But, yes, we do have a room. Looks like I have two left. Would you like one on the other side of the courtyard or by the street?

ISAAC

By the street is fine.

ISAAC EXITS and SAMUEL ENTERS. SAMUEL looks like he could be SAM'S twin.

SAMUEL

Shalom, my son. I am Samuel, from Jerusalem.

DANIEL

Wow, that's quite a costume you have there!

SAMUEL

I wear these in hopes that the Romans will give me at least some respect. I am a Rabbi with the Hillel synagogue.

DANIEL

Well, Rabbi you must have been saying your prayers. You get the last room.

SAMUEL

Many thanks my son. And to He who watches over Israel.

DANIEL

Where are you parked?

SAMUEL

Parked?

DANIEL

Er...how did you get here?

SAMUEL

Ahhh. No, I have no camel, or donkey. I have made the journey on foot.

DANIEL

Well...okay. Your room is through the courtyard and to the left.

DANIEL moves around the counter to assist SAMUEL with his bag.

SAMUEL

That's all right. I am not so old yet that I can't handle my own bags. I will find my own way.

DANIEL

Dinner's at six.

SAMUEL

Six? You should say the twelfth hour. You have been around these Romans too much for you to say six o'clock.

SAMUEL EXITS.

DANIEL

What on earth has Sarah done? I think I need to have a talk with that woman.

LIGHTS FADE OUT.

<u>SONG</u>

<u>SONG</u>

Scene 5

LIGHTS COME UP.

SARAH is sweeping the dust off the floor. DANIEL ENTERS from stage left.

DANIEL

This place is jam packed. What on earth have you done?

SARAH

Daniel, would you do me a favor? Would you check on that young couple in the stable? She is quite large with her child. If I am not mistaken her time is well nigh near.

DANIEL

The stable? What are they doing out there?

SARAH

Well, was I supposed to just turn them out in the streets. It is chaos out there with every inn full...and that poor young girl...such a long journey. And what a time to have to travel. I thought surely we could do something. At least we could offer them the stable, until a room opens up.

DANIEL

All right, all right...I'll check on them. But when I get back we really need to talk about all this *(Turns back)*. Oh...what..uh...what are their names?

SARAH

You should ask. What were they? Her's was... Mary....and his was Joseph. From Nazareth. They were the sweetest couple. Mind you, not the slightest complaint about their situation. In fact, they were so thankful you'd think we'd given them our finest room.

DANIEL turns to leave but stops just as he reaches the door.

DANIEL

Wait a minute. Did you say their names were Mary and Joseph?

SARAH

Yes, from Nazareth. Why?

DANIEL

Forget it. Forget it. I'm not even going to go down that road.

DANIEL heads out the door muttering on the way.

DANIEL

This I have to see.

LIGHTS FADE DOWN.

<u>SONG</u>

<u>SONG</u>

Scene 6

LIGHTS COME UP.

The GUESTS are seated around a low table preparing for the evening meal.

ISAAC

My question to you is where is it written that these Romans should rule over Israel?

DANIEL and SARAH ENTER carrying bowls of bread. They begin to serve the food.

SAMUEL

It says in the Book of Books that God watches over the ways of man. He knows that we are suffering.

DANIEL

(Aside to SARAH)

Wait 'til he tries Ruth's cooking. Then he'll really know suffering.

ISAAC

If you ask me, bless His Holy name, the Lord is doing too much watching and not enough doing.

RUTH ENTERS carrying food. DANIEL hurries to take the plate from her so that he can examine the food.

DANIEL

What's this?

RUTH

Can't you tell?

DANIEL

If I could tell, would I be asking you what it is?

RUTH

It's called Rachel's fig delight.

DANIEL

Those are figs? Here. Uh... I'll take it from here.

RUTH EXITS.

BENJAMIN

All I can say is if He watches over us much longer, He will watch the Romans tax me right out of my camel and my house.

DANIEL

If you think your taxes are bad you should see the taxes I have to pay back home.

SAMUEL

Is not your home here, in Bethlehem?

DANIEL

Not really. Uh....it's a long story.

BENJAMIN

Good Rabbi, now that our host is here, perhaps you will honor us with the prayer.

SAMUEL

Of course. *(Lifts hands)* Hear O Israel the Lord thy God is One. O Lord we thank you for bringing us to this place safely and we thank you for your endless mercy. We are also thankful for this meal and for our host. Hear us O Lord as we give thanks to you for the promise of a Messiah. We pray that He may come soon...very soon. Amen

BENJAMIN

For those who have caused us to come here...perhaps we are not so thankful?

SAMUEL

God in His providence knows what is best. Let us look forward and be ready for when the Chosen One comes.

ISAAC

Rabbi, with all due respect, surely you don't suggest that the Messiah will be here soon. We've been waiting for centuries. Are you aware of some sign of His coming?

SAMUEL

No. I have not seen a sign. But when it happens...God will make sure that we know. We will not have to guess. There will be some sort of clear sign.

SARAH ENTERS and motions to DANIEL to hurry so that the food will not get cold.

DANIEL

Rabbi, I have seen a sign that leaves no doubt...that it is time to eat.

LIGHTS FADE OUT.

SONG

SONG

Scene 7

LIGHTS COME UP.

SARAH ENTERS carrying a water jar. She sets it down and ladles some water into a smaller container. DANIEL ENTERS.

DANIEL

There you are. I think its time we had a little talk.

SARAH

First tell me what you think of the child.

DANIEL

You mean...in the stable?

SARAH

Of course.

DANIEL

(Collecting his thoughts)

Well...he's...different. I can't quite put my finger on it. He's so...peaceful. That's it. Like he's totally content. You know, I haven't heard him cry once yet.

DANIEL's attention has been caught by an object he sees out the open window.

SARAH

(As she's leaving)

That is a special child. Mark my words. Woman's intuition.

DANIEL

Woman's intuition. You always say that. Okay. So's he's a good baby. Have you noticed this star? Sarah? Sarah?

THREE SHEPHERDS come barreling through the door. They are a "rag tag" group, unkempt, excited, and out-of-breath.

REUBEN

Sir, we are looking for the baby...

SIMEON

...born today in a manger.

MORDECAI

...that the angels told us about.

DANIEL

All right, that's it. I've had enough. Sarah....SARAH.

SARAH

What on earth is the matter?

DANIEL

Look, I think I've played along pretty well with...this. But I've had it. This is the last straw. Now, these "shepherds" want to see the baby out in the stable?

SARAH

Well why don't you show them? *(To shepherds)* He really is the most adorable little baby.

REUBEN

Did the angel speak to you, too?

SIMEON

There was...an army of angels....

MORDECAI

...more than you could count...

SIMEON

...they were singing...singing praises to God.

DANIEL

Oh, sure. Why not?

SAMUEL, BENJAMIN and ISAAC ENTER.

SAMUEL

What is the meaning of this commotion?

DANIEL

They think they have seen angels.

REUBEN

We did. And they said that we would find a baby in the manger.

MORDECAI

...They said He is the Savior.....the Annointed One.

SIMEON

...and that he was just born here in the City of David, this day.

DANIEL

Surely you don't think that this is true?

SAMUEL

It is possible. Micah says, "But you Bethlehem, though you are small among the clans of Judah, out of you will come for me one who will be ruler over Israel"

BENJAMIN

In Bethlehem? This dump? Why would God send the Messiah to be born in a place like this? The best thing to ever come out of Bethlehem is the road to Jerusalem.

SAMUEL

Who are we to question the ways of the Lord? I would like to see this child. Sarah perhaps you can show us the way.

ALL EXIT.

LIGHTS FADE OUT.

<u>SONG</u>

Scene 8

LIGHTS COME UP.

DANIEL

You know that star is starting to give me the creeps. It seems like its been right overhead now for weeks. It's so bright it's hard to get to sleep.

SARAH

That is not just a star, Daniel. It is a sign from God.

DANIEL

Let me guess. Woman's intuition. Sarah. I know that there have been some strange and wonderful things going on here. I mean, I can't explain how those shepherds knew that the child had been born here. I can't explain how that baby is so peaceful. It's amazing. He almost has a glow about him. But what I really can't understand is how these people are coming from all over to see him. It's bizarre. But it sure has been great for business. We've never done this well!

RUTH ENTERS.

RUTH

Come quick, there is a great caravan coming! They are Magi from the east. They are looking for the child!

DANIEL

A large caravan?

RUTH

Huge. More camels than I can count.

DANIEL

Now that is a sign from God. This child has been great for business. Ruth, what are you waiting for? Run to find the leader of the caravan. Bring 'em here. Go, go.

RUTH rushes out.

DANIEL

Don't forget to tell them we have plenty of room. *(To Sarah)* We can get rid of these other guys.

SARAH

Daniel. That child is a miracle from God. Not some....thing...for you to make a profit.

DANIEL

Ah...Sarah. Maybe that's why God sent the child here? To help us out. How 'bout that, huh?

SARAH

I have been watching these strange and wonderful events and I know that this child is from God. Whether He is the Chosen One or the Savior I do not know.

But I for one believe that God has sent this child to be with us for a reason. And it's not for you to make some money.

SARAH angrily EXITS.

DANIEL

Ah...Sarah. What did I say this time?

LIGHTS FADE OUT.

SONG

SONG - WE THREE KINGS - *During the song, Daniel follows the Magi to the manger where he begins to experience the joy of the Magi as they come to worship the Child.*

LIGHTS FADE OUT as the magi leave the stage.

Scene 9

LIGHTS COME UP.

DANIEL awakens lying on a mat. He is back in the lobby of the bed and breakfast in Osprey. SAM, and IKE are all standing nearby, while SARAH is applying a moist towel to his head.

SARAH

Dan, Dan...can you hear me?

DAN

Where am I?

SARAH

You're at home.

DAN

Home? You mean I'm not in Bethlehem any more?

SARAH

Bethlehem? *(Laughs)* Oh, no Dan. You're home...in Florida. You were knocked out cold.

IKE

Uh...sorry, Dan. It was an accident. You know with the ladder.

DAN

Oh...the ladder. Its coming back to me. I must have had a dream. But...but it seemed so real. And Ike...you were in it. All of you were in it. We were at an inn int...Bethlehem. But it wasn't just any inn in Bethlehem. It was THE inn... you know, the one at the very first Christmas, where Jesus was born. And all of you guys were there. Ike was a....carpenter. And Sam...you were a rabbi.

SAM

Well...mazel toff.

SARAH

I probably wasn't even in it.

DAN

(Hugs SARAH)

You were my loving wife, as always.

SARAH

And don't you forget it.

DAN

The weird part was that I actually saw Mary and Joseph and the baby...Jesus. Just like the story goes in the Bible.

IKE

You're kidding me, right? I'm surprised you even know the story. *(DAN grimaces at IKE) (IKE holds hands up)* Just kidding, just kidding.

DAN

I saw the Shepherds...you know who the angels spoke to, and the star...I...I saw everything. The best part was when the magi came...you know the wise men. Because then I realized something that I never realized before. As I watched them give those gifts at that very first Christmas I began to realize that Jesus Himself was a gift...for us. It all began to make sense to me. I mean how else could we really begin to understand God unless He came into our world and became like one of us? Because then for the first time we could really start to understand God, because we could actually see Him, and we could...we could talk to Him and we...

SARAH

(Moves close to hug DAN)

...we could become close to Him.

DAN

Yes...exactly. I understand all that now.

SAM

Well...are you ready? Are you finally ready to become a...believer?

DAN

Am I ready? *(Pauses)* Yes! Yes, think I am ready. I'd like to start a new life...a life as a believer.

SAM

(High fives DAN)

Hallelujah, brother!

DAN

I think I need to start by asking each of you to forgive me. I haven't always been the best husband...or friend...or employer. Can you do that?

SAM

Of course.

IKE

Sure.

SARAH

I'll always forgive you.

SAM

Dan, this is a miracle. I've been hoping and praying for this day for a long time. I can't tell you how happy I am for you.

SARAH

I'm so happy. I knew...that some day this time would come.

DAN

Let me guess...woman's intuition?

SARAH

Yes. I guess you could say that.

RUTH ENTERS.

RUTH

Oh. He's awake.

DAN

Don't sound so enthusiastic.

RUTH

I was just surprised. Hey! I made something for everyone to try.

SARAH

Um...great...Ruth. Whad'ya make?

RUTH

It's a surprise.

DAN

Smells familiar. Let me see. *(Walks over to RUTH)* Ah...its Rachel's Fig Delight.

RUTH

Mr. Shephard? How did you know that? I've never made this before.

DAN

(Drapes arm around RUTH'S shoulder)

It's uh...it's a long story. Why don't I tell you the whole thing at dinner?

RUTH

Well...I'd better get started on dinner right away.

DAN

Wait...wait...uh... I have an idea! Why don't we all go out to dinner?

ALL

Yeah, yeah. Right. Good idea.

ALL EXIT.

LIGHTS FADE OUT.

MESSAGE

<u>SONG</u>

<u>SONG</u>

The Red Bible

By Skip Martin

<u>SONG</u>

<u>SONG</u>

Scene 1

LIGHTS COME ON.

PAUL LOHSE quietly enters carrying a large package wrapped in brown paper. He looks around nervously for a moment for a place to put it. Finally, he decides to put in next to the couch where it is discretely out of view, but not hidden.

CATHY

Paul? Is that you?

PAUL

No. It's just the neighborhood burglar stopping in for a visit.

CATHY enters stage left.

CATHY

You know how I feel about sarcasm. I wished you wouldn't do that.

PAUL

It's not sarcasm, Cathy. It's called a sense of humor. Surely we're permitted to have a sense of humor these days.

CATHY

Only if we are in a situation which calls for humor. Which we most definitely are not.

As CATHY moves past the couch she notices the package.

CATHY

Oh, no...Paul what is this? What did you buy? I thought we agreed not spend any more money.

PAUL

Yes. I know, we did. But this is something special. It's one of a kind. It's...

CATHY

You always say that. It's always something isn't it? Paul, haven't we been over this over and over again? We have no money. We can't pay our bills. We have no money for Christmas. I can't believe you bought that!

PAUL

Don't you want to know what it is?

CATHY

No. I don't want to know! I don't want to know. I'm so angry with you right now. *(Crosses over to get her purse)* What is it?

PAUL walks over to package and gently unwraps it.

PAUL

(Smiling)

It's a Bible.

CATHY

A Bible? Why on earth did you have to buy a Bible?

PAUL

Cathy. This Bible is priceless. Look....it was printed in 1720. It's an original by William Coverdale There can't be many of these still around....

CATHY

Great. Just great. And just how much did you spend on this...*Bible*?

PAUL

Look...honey...I know you'll think it's a lot. But...it's really not. Not when you consider how valuable it is...

CATHY

...oh...no...how much?

PAUL

It was only four hundred and fifty dollars...

CATHY

...four hundred and fifty dollars! You spent four hundred and fifty on a stupid Bible. How could you do that? We don't even have four hundred and fifty dollars. I don't believe this! That's it. That's it. I'm outta here.

CATHY storms out stage right.

PAUL

Cathy...Cathy...CAT...T...THY. Oh, boy...oh...well. *(Looks up)* Lord, I sure hope you have a plan for this marriage because things look pretty bad around here and there are not too many positions open for divorced marriage counselors.

PAUL walks over and picks up the RED BIBLE.

PAUL

Ah...man. This was such a good deal

PAUL slumps down on the couch with the RED BIBLE and opening it, begins reading the inside cover.

PAUL

"William Coverdale, printer. 1720". Hmn. What's this? A pocket?

PAUL pulls out several ancient letters, blows the dust off of one and begins examining it.

PAUL

I, William Coverdale, have printed this Bible on the occasion of the birth of my first child. It is my hope, dear reader, that you will obtain as much profit as I from the reading of this, the greatest of all books. I would be most pleased if before you part ways with this book that you might set a letter in your own hand and add it to this one in the pocket of my own design." Wow that's incredible! Cathy....CATHY! You should...see...this.. Oh...she's gone. *(There is a long pause. Then PAUL speaks to the Bible)* Bet you've seen a lot of things. Got any good advice for me?

LIGHTS FADE OUT.

<u>SONG</u>

<u>SONG</u>

Scene 2

LIGHTS COME UP.

SALLY COVERDALE ENTERS and carefully bustles about her small tidy home. She cheerfully hums her favorite hymn, even though she appears to be near the end of her pregnancy.

She jumps with a start as WILLIAM COVERDALE loudly enters.

SALLY

William! You startled me. I have been worried about you. What kept you so late?

WILLIAM

I have been working on a very special project. The likes of which you have never seen before. This is a masterpiece. Truly a masterpiece.

SALLY

Indeed? A masterpiece. That is surprising coming from you. You are not easily pleased.

WILLIAM

Well this....this pleases me very much. It is very special. In fact...it is a birthday present. A most grand birthday present.

SALLY

Is that so? And whose birthday might it be that has you working so late?

WILLIAM

(Walking to Sally and placing his hand on her belly) Well whom do you think? A very special present can only be for a very special child.

SALLY

(With realization)

Oh...you mean...Oh, William. You are so thoughtful. I was beginning to wonder. You have spent so much time down at the shop.

WILLIAM

Yes..I know, I know. I have been gone far too much. But this was worth it. Come...would you like to see it?

SALLY

What do you think? Of course I would like to see it.

WILLIAM

Wait right here. I have it right outside.

WILLIAM strides to the door, steps out for a moment, and then returns with a rather large RED BIBLE.

WILLIAM

Well...what do you think?

SALLY

This....book. This is what you have spent so much time working on?

WILLIAM

This book...as you call it...is not just any book, Sally. This is the Holy Bible... in the King's good English. Authorized by King James himself. Sally do you not see? Now...anyone who wants to read the Scriptures for himself need only open the cover and...it is all there. The very words of God for the understanding of the common man.

SALLY

But why would anyone want to read it themselves...is that not what the good reverend is for?

WILLIAM

Sally. If the reverend reads God's word on the Sabbath day, then only the people whom are present will learn the Word. With this Bible and others like it, many more people may learn God's word. Perhaps, God willing, some day long after you and I are gone, someone will be able to open this book and they will be able to know the Word of God.

SALLY starts to walk back to the hearth.

SALLY

That is lovely.

WILLIAM

Wait...there is something else...special about this.

SALLY

What? What is it?

WILLIAM

Come let me show you.

SALLY crosses back over to WILLIAM.

WILLIAM

See....here...?

SALLY

A pocket? A pocket...in a Bible? What on earth for?

WILLIAM

For us...for them...whomever might come to possess it. Do you not see? We can place in here a letter. Perhaps we might set down on paper a word about us, our dreams....our child. Then, sometime, someone after us may do the same. Think of it! We can speak to someone who may live 100 years from now. Just as this Bible speaks to us from so many years ago.

SALLY

That is wonderful...for people like you who can read. But what of the rest of us? How will we learn God's word?

WILLIAM

Someone will read it to them...as I to you. Come....sit you with me for a while.

WILLIAM and SALLY move to two stools near the fireplace.

WILLIAM

Here...St. Matthew. *(He reads Matthew 1: 18-21 and Matthew 1: 22-23)*

SALLY

It is a beautiful story. And that is the most beautiful Red Bible upon which I have ever laid eyes.

WILLIAM

Thank you dear Madam. I hold your words to my heart with much esteem. *(Pauses)* Sally...listen to me....there is something that I have never told you. You must know...this Bible is even more special than you know. You see for twenty five years I prayed for us to have a child. But there was nothing...no answer... only silence. First, I shouted....then I railed against the Lord....

SALLY

I know.

WILLIAM

Yes. For that I am sorry...but...I realized my anger was hurting only myself. So...I began to thank God anyways, for all that He had given me. Then to honor His Blessed Son, I dedicated myself to making this Bible. Sally...well...I can not explain this. But within weeks....you told me that you were with child.

SALLY

William...does not the Book say that "He will honour those who honour Him?"

WILLIAM

It does indeed. This Bible....is a testament to God's blessing to us.

SALLY

(Taking William's hands)

For that I thank Him and you. Come. Let us sup. Those people three hundred years from now will simply have to wait.

LIGHTS FADE OUT.

<u>SONG</u>

<u>SONG</u>

<u>SONG</u>

Scene 3

LIGHTS COME UP to reveal PRUDENCE MARTIN sweeping the main room of her cabin.

ISRAEL MARTIN wearily walks in, places his musket and powder satchel by the door, and plops down on a three legged stool. He is totally lost in his thoughts.

PRUDENCE

Well...dear husband. Is it now the custom in the Martin household for the husband to enter his homestead without slightest nod or greeting for his dear wife?

ISRAEL

What? What was that you said?

PRUDENCE

I said that King George was just here and wanted to know how you were doing.

ISRAEL

Oh...go on with you. Funnin' with your husband in his time of trouble.

PRUDENCE

Oh...I'm terribly sorry. I didn't realize that the entire fate of these colonies rested on your shoulders.

ISRAEL

Go on....go on...joke if you must. But this is serious business that is going on around us. All this drillin' we're doing out on the commons means just one thing Prudence. There's going to be a war. And war is not a very pretty thing.

PRUDENCE

Oh...surely it won't come to that?

ISRAEL

Well I can assure you that the King didn't send all those Redcoats to Boston just for a Sabbath Day picnic.

PRUDENCE

And surely they will return to England once they see to it that all the proper taxes and duties are collected.

ISRAEL

I don't think so. I 'spect sometime in the spring those Redcoats will come marching out this way, Prudence. I'm afraid of what might happen to our town...to us...to you.

PRUDENCE

Well, I thank you for your concern, sir. But you need not worry about me, or us, or this town.

ISRAEL

How so?

PRUDENCE

Come...let us see what the scriptures say. *(PRUDENCE gets up and taking ISRAEL by the hand takes him over to where she has left the RED BIBLE)* It's right here in St. Matthew. "Take therefore no thought for the morrow; for the morrow shall take thought for the things of itself. Sufficient unto the day is the evil thereof."

ISRAEL

Speaks to the heart doesn't it.

PRUDENCE

As mine does to you.

ISRAEL

You're a good wife, Prudence. I thank God for you every day *(They embrace)*

CHARLOTTE enters stage left, and seeing her parents hug, rushes to join them.

CHARLOTTE

Me too, me too.

THE MARTINS all laugh.

ISRAEL

Charlotte, I want you to promise me somethin'?

CHARLOTTE

What daddy?

ISRAEL

Someday, if anything ever happens to your mum, or to me, I want you to promise to take this Red Bible and make sure that nothing ever happens to it. Will you promise me that?

CHARLOTTE

Of course, papa, I won't ever let anything happen to it. Not ever.

ISRAEL

I know you won't. I know you won't. And the special pocket. Don't forget the pocket. You'll want to put your letter in there...just like the others.

CHARLOTTE

Of course, papa. And I already know what mine will be about.

ISRAEL

And do you mind me askin' what that might be?

CHARLOTTE

It's going to be about my very favorite thing in the whole world.

ISRAEL

Oh..it's about me?

CHARLOTTE

Papa...don't be so silly. It's going to be about Christmas.

PRUDENCE

Tomorrow is Christmas Day you know.

ISRAEL

Surely, you jest.

PRUDENCE

I jest not. You have been much too busy to take note.

ISRAEL

Well then... I must beg your pardon. And I say that now is as good a time as any to take note. Charlotte, can you fetch your father the Bible?

CHARLOTTE rushes over to the Red Bible and struggles to hand it to her father.

ISRAEL

Let's see. I think we will find the appropriate reading in St. Luke. Here it... is. Found it. *(ISRAEL reads Luke 2:8-12 and then PRUDENCE reads Luke 2:13-14)*

CHARLOTTE

Then the shepherds got to go see baby Jesus. That's not fair. I wish I could see baby Jesus.

ISRAEL

But you shall Charlotte. You shall. You see...one day you will pass from this world and join all who believe in the Blessed Savior in meeting Him.

CHARLOTTE

I can't wait. I can't wait!

PRUDENCE

Well we rather hope that you stay with us for quite a while yet.

CHARLOTTE

(Smiling)

I guess so.

ISRAEL

Well...there. Thanks to you both, I feel like a much better man. Charlotte would you put the Bible in its place? Madam, would you do me the honour of joining me for walk on the commons? It is Christmas you know.

PRUDENCE

My dear Isreal, I thought you'd never notice. And the answer is...yes; the honour would be mine, sir.

CHARLOTTE

Me too, me too!

PRUDENCE and ISRAEL join arms while CHARLOTTE takes ISRAEL's hand as they march off stage right.

LIGHTS FADE OUT.

<u>SONG</u>

<u>SONG</u>

Scene 4

LIGHTS COME UP.

CATHY slowly enters and looks around.

CATHY

Paul...PAUL. Are you home? Paul...I'm...sorry.

CATHY starts to put her things away when she notices the RED BIBLE. Curious she opens it, and finds the pocket and several of the letters. She dusts one off and begins reading it.

CATHY

My name is Charlotte. I am ten years old. My very favorite thing in the whole world is Christmas. I hope that yours is too. Christmas is the birthday of Jesus. Jesus was God's Son. The Magi came and brought special gifts to Jesus. Children receive gifts on Christmas too and that's why I think it is so fun. But the best thing of all about Christmas was God's gift. It was Jesus. I hope that anyone who reads this will remember all about Christmas.

Putting down the letter, CATHY begins to cry.

CATHY

Oh..Paul. I'm sorry. I'm sorry. I'm so sorry.

LIGHTS FADE OUT.

SONG

SONG

Scene 5

LIGHTS COME UP.

JAMES OWENS enters with a frown on his face.

JAMES

Winnifred? Winnifr.e.e.ed? Have you seen my pipe?

WINNIFRED OWENS briskly ENTERS as she is pulling off her gloves. She is dressed in the latest fashion of 1903; wearing a broad hat with flowers, and a long flowing dress. She is also wearing a sash on which is printed the words: Women Deserve the Vote

WINNIFRED

It's on the table right by your Bible dear. Right where you always put it.

JAMES

No...no. Right where *you* always put it. I always put over there next to my chair.

WINNIFRED

Well...James...it doesn't belong by the chair. It belongs on the table. Honestly...I don't know why you can't remember that.

JAMES

(Rolling eyes)

Haberdash.

JAMES gets his pipe and sits down.

JAMES

Dear...I really don't understand why you insist on spending so much of your time pursuing this woman's....vote. After all, your place is here...in the home. And besides, what on earth would women do if they should ever get the vote? Which, of course, they never will. Good heavens, can you just imagine all of the utter nonsense that would begin to come out of the politicians' mouths just to please women.

WINNIFRED

First of all, we shall win the right to vote, and we *shall* exercise the right to vote every bit as well as you *men* have. And second, thank you to the many modern conveniences of life, of which you yourself so often boast, I find that I can handle quite well my responsibilities here at home and still be able to help all of my sisters in need.

JAMES

Yes, yes. You handle it all quite well. I suppose that now you shall want to start wearing pants and smoke cigars.

WINNIFRED

Oh, nonsense, James, I can't imagine how any woman in her right mind should ever want to do such a thing. (*Looks at James in puzzlement)* James, you're jealous aren't you?

JAMES

What? Jealous? Oh, don't be silly. Me....jealous? What on earth would I be jealous about?

WINNIFRED

Independence. You're afraid that I might become an independent woman. That you won't be needed anymore.

JAMES

Oh...don't be daft.

WINNIFRED

No...no. That's it! That's it. *(Approaches James*) My dear sweet James is worried about losing his witty....strong... yet very faithful and adoring wife.

JAMES

Oh...come now.

WINNIFRED

James...I shall always want you and need you no matter how strong or independent that I may appear. You shall always have my undying love.

JAMES
(Hugging Winnifred)
Oh...blast it all. You always seem to know how to melt my heart.

WINNIFRED
That's why God created women.

JAMES
(Breaking away)
But...but...there's still something not quite right. Something is being lost in all this. What about tradition? Is there something wrong with that? Why can't we simply do things in the traditional way?

WINNIFRED
There's absolutely nothing wrong with tradition. You shall always have your traditional chair by the fire...your pipe in its place on the table. You shall always have your traditional seat at the head of the dinner table and you shall say your traditional prayer...

JAMES
...yes...yes...well...thank you. I suppose...when it seems that everything is changing. Sometimes one just needs to know that some things will still stay the same.

WINNIFRED
It's Christmas Eve James. Shouldn't we call the children together for our family tradition?

JAMES
Yes...yes..of course. You're quite right. *(Walks stage right)* WILBUR.... KATHERINE...come here please. It's time.

KATHERINE and WILBUR OWENS rush in excitedly from stage right.

WILBUR
Can we open presents now?

KATHERINE
Yes...yes. Can we?

JAMES
In a few moments. But first we shall take a few minutes to remember the meaning of the season. As you know, it is a tradition in our family to read from

the family Bible which has been passed down for some time. Katherine....would you like the honor of getting out the Red Bible?

KATHERINE

Yes...father.

KATHERINE walks over and gets the Red Bible out from it's place in a small chest by the hearth.

JAMES

All right...everybody gather around. I should like to read one of my favorite verses from St. Luke. *(James reads LUKE 2: 25-32)*

JAMES

Wilbur...Katherine. I hope you will carry on this tradition with your families when you get older

KATHERINE

Yes, father.

WILBUR

Yes, father.

WINNIFRED

And don't forget that Jesus is the reason for the season.

JAMES

I rather like that Winnie. Did you think of that yourself?

KATHERINE

Yes, Mother. That rhymes.

WINNIFRED

I guess I did?

WILBUR

Can we open presents now?

JAMES

Winnie?

WINNIFRED

Why not.

WILBUR and KATHERINE

Hooray. Yeah.

As the CHILDREN rush offstage, JAMES and KATHERINE link arms together and start to follow them.

JAMES

I'll have to tell that Ben in the print shop. We might be able to do something with that. Jesus..is the reason for the season? Yes...people might like that.

LIGHTS FADE OUT.

SONG

SONG

Scene 6

LIGHTS COME UP.

JIMMY WEBSTER enters carrying his suitcase. He is dressed in his best Army dress uniform as he stands before the mirror and carefully places his hat in just the right spot on his neatly combed head.

JIMMY

Maggie...are you ready?

There is no answer.

JIMMY

Maggie are you ready? The train leaves in just an hour. *(Pauses)* MAGGIE?

MAGGIE briskly walks in, still making final adjustments to her hair.

MAGGIE

Don't get cross Jimmy. I want to look my best for you. I don't....I don't know when you'll see me again.

JIMMY

You look like an angel darlin'...an absolute angel. And don't you go worryin' 'bout me now. I'll be back. I will. It'll be sooner than you think.

MAGGIE

Jimmy...you know very well that's not true..It could be a year...or even more.... or...*(Starts crying)*

JIMMY goes to comfort MAGGIE with a hug.

JIMMY

Sweetheart...everything's going to be all right. It's gonna be all right.

MAGGIE

I know...I know. But I wish you didn't have to go. I wish this blasted war would just go away. I wish I'd never heard of Pearl Harbor.

JIMMY

I know...I know...

MAGGIE

....and why do you have to go at Christmas of all times?

JIMMY

Maggie...the Army doesn't have holidays. *(Long pause)* You've got the Bible? You'll promise me you'll take care of it....no matter what?

MAGGIE

Yes...yes..of course. You don't need to worry about it.

JIMMY

Well you know 'ole Aunt Winnie would 'probably come back from the grave to kill me if anything ever happened to it.

MAGGIE

(Laughing)

She probably would.

JIMMY

(Looks at watch)

We've got just a few minutes. Let's read some scriptures.

MAGGIE

Why of course Jimmy.

JIMMY

(Leafing through Bible)

Being it's Christmas and all...and me goin' on this journey...I was thinking of the story of the Magi. *(JIMMY reads Matt. 2:1, MAGGIE reads Matt.2:9-11)*

JIMMY

I don't have gold or frankincense or myrrh....but I do have this.

JIMMY hands a small carefully wrapped box to MAGGIE. MAGGIE unwraps it, revealing a silver heart necklace.

JIMMY

I hope you like it.

MAGGIE

It's lovely. It's absolutely beautiful.

JIMMY

(Demonstrates)

It opens like this. See. I...uh...put my picture inside.

MAGGIE

I'll open it every day you're gone.

MAGGIE opens her purse.

MAGGIE

I have a gift for you too.

JIMMY opens his package to reveal a small pocket watch.

JIMMY

A pocket watch. Oh...that's swell. It's a beaut. It's a real beaut.

MAGGIE

It has a picture inside also.

JIMMY

(Joking)

Of me?

MAGGIE lightly slugs JIMMY.

MAGGIE

No...you big goof.

JIMMY

(Opening watch to see picture)

(Whistles with delight) Wow! Maggie it almost captures how truly beautiful you are.

MAGGIE

Oh? Flattery will get you everywhere.

THEY laugh and then hug again.

JIMMY

Did you set the time?

MAGGIE

Yes. I did it yesterday.

JIMMY

Well...then it's time to go. Merry Christmas. I love you.

MAGGIE

Merry Christmas. I love you too.

Hand in hand MAGGIE and JIMMY EXIT stage right.

LIGHTS FADE OUT.

SONG

SONG

Scene 7

LIGHTS COME UP.

PAUL ENTERS and takes off his jacket. He looks around and sees that CATHY has left some things on the coffee table.

PAUL

Cathy....are you home?

CATHY enters, relieved that PAUL is back.

CATHY

There you are. Look...I need to talk to you. I...I...I apologize for the way I acted. I don't know what happened to me. I guess...its just the financial stress we're under right now....it must have triggered something. Look... I've decided that if that Bible is that important to you...you can...keep it.

PAUL

Cathy. It wasn't that important. I know I shouldn't have spent that kind of money without asking you. So...I'm the one who should apologize. I guess...y'know because it was such a rare find and the price was so unbelievable...well..I just didn't want to pass the opportunity by.

CATHY

You never pass the opportunity to buy. That's the problem. *(Pauses to take a deep breath)* Okay. I said I'm sorry. I don't want to fight anymore..and well... it's Christmas Eve. We don't have any money...but it's Christmas Eve.

PAUL

I accept your apology

PAUL and CATHY embrace.

PAUL

We actually do have some money.

CATHY

Really?

PAUL pulls a wad of cash out of his pocket.

PAUL

In fact...we've got two hundred and fifty dollars..

CATHY

How?

PAUL

After I saw how upset you were....I decided to take the Bible back. At first the shopkeeper wouldn't take it back. But I kept begging him...I told him it might save me from getting divorced...so...then finally he agreed.

CATHY

Paul. I would never divorce you. I might kill you.... but never divorce you. Seriously... no matter what I would never do that. But...didn't the Bible cost four hundred and fifty dollars? What happened to the other two hundred?

PAUL

Two hundred fifty is all he would give me for it. Said he had a business to run and it was take it or leave it. So...I took it.

CATHY

I can't believe that. That's highway robbery. *(Pauses)* Paul...you didn't have to take it back. But I appreciate the thought. At least you got the two fifty.

PAUL

Here...I'm going to let you have the money. I don't know if I can trust myself with it.

CATHY

(Quickly takes money)

Good idea.

PAUL

Hey. Aren't you at least supposed to put up a fight?

CATHY

(With a smile)

Not when it comes to you and money.

PAUL

(Holds up hands)

All right...all right.

CATHY

Listen...I've got to run a few errands. Can you mow the lawn before you watch the game?

PAUL

What lawn? Oh...you mean the weeds and dirt in the front of the house.

CATHY

(With some exasperation)

Yes. Mr. Smarty Pants. Bye.

CATHY EXITS.

LIGHTS FADE OUT.

<u>SONG</u>

<u>SONG</u>

Scene 8

LIGHTS COME UP.

PAUL and CATHY ENTER.

CATHY

Well...that was quite a Christmas dinner.

PAUL

Yeah...don't think I've ever had Christmas dinner at Checkers before.

CATHY

You know....honestly...going to a fancy restaurant really isn't that important to me. What's important is that we had some special time together.

PAUL

I guess so.

CATHY

You know. I'm glad we went to that Christmas Eve service. And the sermon really spoke to me.

PAUL

Yeah. Can you believe that the minister finished in nineteen minutes? That's got to be a church record.

CATHY

(Annoyed)

Paul!

PAUL

Well...he did. I timed it.

CATHY

(Even more annoyed)

Paul!

PAUL

All right. All right.

CATHY

I want to talk about it. It was a special moment for me.

PAUL

Okay. I'm listening.

CATHY

It was that thing he said about scientist and the anthill. I never thought of Christmas that way before.

PAUL

I guess I missed that part. Remember? I was out in the parking lot turning off the car lights.

CATHY

Oh yeah. Sorry. Well...he told a story about a scientist who wanted to study an anthill in his garden. Each time the scientist approached the hill, the ants would scurry away in terror. How could he let the ants know that he had only good will and did not wish them any harm? If only he could communicate with them he thought; but then he realized that even that wouldn't be enough. They would never believe he understood their problems, their struggle for food, their battles with other ants.

PAUL

Is there a point to all this?

CATHY

I'm getting there. Okay. So, finally he decided that only one thing could give them complete confidence. If only by some miracle he could - for a time- become an ant. *(Pauses)* Then it hit me. Right between the eyes. I understood it for the first time.

PAUL

(With realization)

Oh. I think I get it too! You mean that was Jesus? God entered our world and became - for a time - just like us.

CATHY

Exactly! Paul...if God loves us that much...can't we trust Him, His motives, His complete goodwill for us?

PAUL

Well...I guess. Theoretically...we should be able to trust Him. With everything. Even with our finances.

CATHY

So...what's holding us back?

PAUL

I guess what holds us back is we don't take the time to get to know Him well enough. So we don't trust Him.

CATHY

Yeah. I think you're right. We spend too much time worrying about other things. Like...

PAUL AND CATHY

Money!

PAUL

Yeah.

CATHY

But...there is a way we could change that?

PAUL

Really. How?

CATHY

You'll find a hint behind the couch.

PAUL

What? What do you mean?

CATHY

Just go look behind the couch.

PAUL

Okay.

PAUL gets up and goes to see what is behind the couch. Puzzled, he bends over to pick up a large brown package.

PAUL

Cathy? What is this? *(Pauses*) Is this what I think it is?

CATHY

(beaming)

You'll see. Open it up.

As PAUL unwraps the package it becomes apparent that it is the RED BIBLE.

PAUL

I don't believe it. What? How did you get it?

CATHY

I went to the store and the owner sold it back to me.

PAUL

But...then you had to spend what was left of that money.

CATHY

Nope. Only fifty. I made him a deal. I told him I wouldn't report him for not collecting the sales tax when he sold it to you the first time.

PAUL laughs.

CATHY

And...he threw in something else in the bargain. (*Gets up to walk over to the fireplace)* This box. Apparently when he first bought the Bible it came in this. Maybe that's why it's still in such good condition.

PAUL

I don't believe it. Why did you......?

CATHY

Before you took the Bible back, I looked at it. I found this letter from a little girl that was written in 1774.

PAUL

You found the pocket!

CATHY

I found the pocket. So anyway, I thought "We really need to keep this Bible". And the rest is history.

PAUL

Did you see the one from Coverdale?

CATHY

No.

PAUL

Well...one of the letters was from the printer... a guy named William Coverdale. In it he said, "It is my hope dear reader that you will obtain as much profit as I from the reading of this, the greatest of all books". Maybe we could profit too?

CATHY

How?

PAUL

By reading the book like all those people before us did.

CATHY

And then someday I could write our letter to put in it.

PAUL

WE can write our letter.

CATHY

All right...all right. You know I'm really glad I have a husband who not only knows a bargain when he sees it, but who also knows a great value.

PAUL

Are you being sarcastic?

CATHY

No dear. It's called the truth.

PAUL

Merry Christmas. I love you.

CATHY

Merry Christmas. I love you too.

LIGHTS FADE OUT.

MESSAGE

<u>SONG</u>

All Rights Reserved

PERFORMANCE RIGHTS AND ROYALTY PAYMENT: All amateur and professional performance rights to this play are controlled exclusively by Skip Martin. No church, amateur or professional production groups or individuals may perform any of the plays in this book without securing license and royalty arrangements in advance. Questions concerning other rights should be addressed to Skip Martin. Appropriate fees will be set upon application in accordance with your producing circumstances. Any licensing requests and inquiries relating to church, amateur and professional performance rights should be addressed to our address on this page. Royalty of the required amount must be paid, whether the play is presented for charity or profit and whether or not admission is charged. In appropriate circumstances, waiver of royalty fees will be considered.

AUTHOR CREDIT: All churches, groups or individuals who receive permission to produce this play must give the author credit in any and all advertisement and publicity relating to the production of this play. The author's billing must appear directly below the title on a separate line where no other written matter appears. The name of the author(s) must be at least 50% as large as the title of the play.

PUBLISHER CREDIT: Whenever this play is produced, all programs, advertisements, flyers or other printed material must include the following notice:

"PRODUCED BY SPECIAL ARRANGEMENT WITH SKIP MARTIN"

APPLICATION: Anyone wishing to arrange for production of A VERY 'JOBIAL' CHRISTMAS, HOLIDAY AT THE INN, IT'S A WONDERFUL CHRISTIAN LIFE, LEAVE IT TO OTTER, SKIPPING CHRISTMAS, THE INNKEEPER'S VISION, THE JOY OF GIVING, THE RED BIBLE, THE SECOND CHANCE, TWO CHRISTMASES, WISE MEN STILL SEEK HIM, or WHERE'S THE LINE FOR JESUS? must make application to Skip Martin, 1620 Main Street, Suite One, Sarasota, Florida 34236, giving the following particulars:

1) Name of the town and the church, theatre or hall in which the proposed production will be presented;
2) The maximum seating capacity of the church, theatre or hall;

3) Scale of ticket prices;
4) The number of performances intended and the dates thereof.

Upon receipt of these particulars you will be provided with the royalty terms and availability.

Royalty and availability quoted on application to Skip Martin, 1620 Main Street, Suite One, Sarasota, Florida 34236. The application may also be faxed to (941) 951-2076 or e-mailed to skip@christmasplays.org.

Performance Royalty Information And Application

If you are planning a production of one of these plays, you must obtain prior written permission from Skip Martin. To obtain a royalty quote, please complete the required portions of this form, and any applicable information for your production. Typically the royalty fee will be fifty dollars ($50) per performance.

All churches, other amateur and or professional groups must complete an application. If you would like a royalty quote or a production license, please complete the following information and sign where applicable. All royalties must be paid in full at least fifteen (15) days prior to the first performance.

Select a Play (one play per Application)

A VERY 'JOBIAL' CHRISTMAS
HOLIDAY AT THE INN
IT'S A WONDERFUL CHRISTIAN LIFE
LEAVE IT TO OTTER
SKIPPING CHRISTMAS
THE INNKEEPER'S VISION
THE JOY OF GIVING
THE RED BIBLE
THE SECOND CHANCE
TWO CHRISTMASES
WISE MEN STILL SEEK HIM
WHERE'S THE LINE FOR JESUS?

Name: ______________________________

Official position: ________________________

Name of producing church or organization: ________________________
Address: ____

City: ______________________ State: __________ Zip: __________

Phone:__________ Fax:__________ Email:______________________

Production Information

Performance dates: ______________________

Tentative number of performances: Minimum __________ Maximum __________

Seating capacity: __________ Expected attendance PER show: __________

Admission price: Adults ______ Seniors ______ Students ______ Children ______

Venue: Location of Performance

Church/Theatre/Building: ______________________

Address: ______________________

City: ______________________ State: __________ Zip: __________

Phone: __________ Fax: __________

Website: ______________________

Signature of Applicant: ______________________ Date: __________

Additional Comments or Questions Regarding this Production

Returning the Application and Obtaining a License

Please return this completed application by mail to: Skip Martin, 1620 Main Street, Suite One, Sarasota, Florida 34236. It may also be faxed to (941) 951-2076 or e-mailed to skip@christmasplays.org. You will then be provided a royalty quote as soon as possible. Upon payment of the appropriate royalties for the play you are performing, you will be provided with a written license.

Skip Martin - 1620 Main Street, Suite One – Sarasota, Florida 34236 – (941) 951-6166

www.christmasplays.org

A Few Words About "Changes" "Adapting"

AND PERFORMING "SCENES FROM" PLAYS

WHAT ARE CHANGES?

All of these plays are protected by international copyright law, which means that any alterations, deletions or substitutions are prohibited by law except with prior written consent of the playwright. Unless expressly noted on the script, any changes made to the script, no matter how minor, must be approved in writing prior to the performance of the play.

WHAT IS AN ADAPTATION?

Adaptations are defined as "making any changes to the text of a play so that it will conform to the requirements or circumstances or limits of your specific production." This includes adding or deleting characters (with the obvious exception of nonspeaking extras) and adding, moving, reassigning and sometimes deleting dialogue. It also includes gender changes. All adaptations must be approved by the author/owner. If you must adapt, send a written request detailing the changes you would like to make at least four weeks in advance of your production. If we require a copy of the script with all of your proposed changes clearly indicated, we will let you know.

WHAT ARE "SCENES FROM" A PLAY?

"Scenes From" applies to whole, unedited excerpts from a play. These may be an act or scene(s) from a play or all of the text from one page through another page. The production must be billed and credited as "Scenes from (Play) by Skip Martin" in all promotional material generated by the Church or producing organization.

QUESTIONS

We hope we've covered everything, but please feel welcome to call us at (941) 951-6166 if you have any questions.

Skip Martin - 1620 Main Street, Suite One – Sarasota, Florida 34236 – (941) 951-6166

www.christmasplays.org

About The Author

Skip Martin lives in Sarasota, Florida with his wife, Beth, to whom he has been married for 27 years. He has a B.S. degree in Economics from Auburn University; a J.D. degree from Florida State University; and a M.F.A degree in Motion Picture, Television, and Recording Arts from Florida State University. Skip is a practicing attorney with several offices in Southwest Florida. He has taught Sunday School to married couples at First Baptist of Sarasota for more than fifteen years, has served the church as a Deacon and Trustee, and helped begin the church's television ministry. For twenty years Skip wrote and directed dramas as part of First Baptist Church's annual presentation of "The Singing Christmas Tree", presenting the good news of the Gift of Christmas in a unique way to more than 10,000 people each year. Skip has also directed/produced two award winning films. Skip is available as a writer, producer and director of church dramas and to write and adapt screenplays.

Printed in the United States
By Bookmasters